Man4 god

G000091315

2015

£2-50

3/22

Christ Will Build His Church

Christ Will Build His Church

But What Is My Role?

Dr. H. Wallace Webster

RESOURCE *Publications* · Eugene, Oregon

CHRIST WILL BUILD HIS CHURCH
But What Is My Role?

Resource Publications
A Division of Wipf and Stock Publishers
199 W. 8th Ave., Suite 3
Eugene, OR 97401

www.wipfandstock.com

ISBN 13: 978-1-55635-954-5

Manufactured in the U.S.A.

Contents

Foreword by Norman L. Geisler vii

Introduction ix

1 Our Story 1

2 Old Testament Mandate 16

3 New Testament Mandate 31

4 Jesus to Peter 48

5 Matthew 28:18–20 55

6 The Early Church Caught It 63

7 The Epistles Taught It 71

8 Paul to Timothy 76

9 1 and 2 Timothy Disciples 85

10 Paul to Others 94

11 Authorities on Disciple-Making 102

12 Expect Opposition 109

13 Shepherding 119

14 The Goal 128

15 The Biggest Obstacle 135

16 Getting Started 144

Bibliography 151

Foreword

THE IMPERATIVE IN THE Great Commission (Matt 28:18–20) is not "go." This is assumed in the original text. The imperative is on "make disciples." And this is the one thing most lacking in the contemporary Christian Church. After speaking in twenty-five countries and fifty states for the last fifty years, I have finally found the solution to this lack of discipleship crisis in the Church.

From the very first moment I walked into Mount Airy Bible Church in Maryland, I could sense something different. There was a solid, stable, and biblical feel about it. When I inquired to find the cause, I found the answer. It was very simple and very biblical: Pastor Wally had personally discipled every man in the church!

When I asked about the program used to do it, I was given several volumes of information. After reviewing it, there was no question in my mind that this had to be made available to other churches. This volume is the result. It is very simply the best I have ever seen—not just on paper, but also in practice—for I have personally observed the lives of the men of Mount Airy Bible Church.

It is no exaggeration to say that this is the most biblical, basic, and successful discipleship training I have ever seen. If every church in the country adopted this material—which they should—it would literally revolutionize the evangelical church. My prayer is that they will adopt it and that it does begin a spiritual revolution in our churches. Charles Spurgeon once wrote an essay that summarizes the condition of way too many churches today. He said, "We are amusing the goats rather than feeding the sheep." Enough with entertainment and back to what the Master commanded: "make disciples." And there is nowhere better to start than with this book.

Norman L. Geisler

Introduction

HAVE YOU EVER BEEN on a mission? When my wife is on a mission, such as shopping, you better stay out of her way. Then why not have a "re-commissioning" or a renewed mission of the church to put us back on a mission for God? Certainly one commission is sufficient, is it not? To this we all must agree, but the purpose of this writing is to rekindle the original commission. Apparently, many churches and pastors have forgotten what Jesus said about the purpose and direction of the church. With today's consumer mentality, it appears that we are more interested in what the community wants instead of what Jesus commissioned. In reality, it has become a neglected call. So what exactly is the neglected call? It is the last command of our Lord, given to His disciples, in which He commanded them to go out and make disciples. This call is clearly meant for us today, and yet it may be one of the most neglected commands in all of Scripture. What is this command, and how do we understand it today? I am amazed at how many Christians are more prone to stand for the Ten Commandments than they are willing to stand for Jesus's commandments, when the Ten Commandments were given to the nation of Israel and the commandments of Jesus are given for the church. Why have we neglected His commands, yet are willing to fight for Israel's commands?

These and other related issues are the subject of this book, with a particular emphasis on men discipling men. I chose this emphasis because this is the journey I have traveled. Every principle discussed can and should be applied to women as well. This is not just a call for men, although it will be addressed from that perspective. Any God-fearing woman can take these principles and apply them to Titus 2 and make an incredible impact for the Kingdom. As a matter of fact, many women are doing so and are making a great difference for the call of Christ. It appears that men are more inclined to be AWOL than the ladies, so this is a wake-up call for men. Sunday school teachers, youth leaders, Christian schools, and other related ministries might also find these thoughts helpful. The goal is clear: we should take Jesus's last command and apply it to all we do for Him. This goal has been neglected, and we need to see that it is necessary. We need to be on a mission!

Ladies, please continue to go forth as you are and maybe even take these thoughts to heart for a deeper commitment to this calling. Please do not see this as some male-dominated theme. This is simply written from a male's perspective because this is the path I have been traveling for these many years. We have a vibrant women's discipleship program in place at our church, but I don't lead this ministry. Maybe we can add this to our second book. Pray that God-fearing men will step up and accept their call. My prayer is the church will awaken to the neglected call—especially the men, who I believe overall are neglecting the call the most.

We will draw our original thoughts from Matthew 28:18–20 where Jesus tells His disciples to go out and make disciples (reproduce themselves). Then we will add 2 Timothy 2:2 for further support of how they understood their call. They found faithful men, and they taught them. We today are the fruit of their endeavors. But will there be a next generation?

There are many people who should be recognized for their support and addition to this work. First and foremost, I want to thank the Lord Jesus for calling me into His Kingdom and giving me the awesome privilege of leading His flock at Mount Airy Bible Church. It has been, and continues to be, a wonderful journey, and I owe it all to Him. Second, I want to thank my family. I left home many evenings to be with the men of the church, and never did my wife complain about the time. She recognized God's call on this ministry and was a tremendous support throughout. She also carefully guided the children so they understood the call. I am thrilled to see how my children have also grasped the call of God on their lives, as they all have given their lives to Jesus and are either serving Him now or preparing to do so. My wife, Vicky, has been an invaluable addition to this work. I also want to thank the men of Mount Airy Bible Church who have labored with me in the task of the development of this ministry. Many of them have labored alongside of me and have been a tremendous blessing. Three men in particular who have labored are Steve Schrader, Patrick Shurney, and Ken Varney. I also want to thank the many wives who have encouraged their husbands to go out on Monday nights to be trained for the call of God.

There are also several editors who deserve special attention. Thanks to Karen Valentine, Dawn Kirk, Kathy Montgomery, Denise Humphrey,

Rebe Schaefer, Ellen Hammond, and Brenda Brown, who have helped oversee this work. Kathy, Ellen, and Denise have especially added their expertise to the PowerPoint presentation of this work.

One final thanks to Mount Airy Bible Church. If more pastors had the privilege to serve at churches like this one, there would be fewer men leaving the ministry. This church has been such a blessing to serve. You have made the call even more of a delight. Thank you to the many who pray, encourage, support, and stand with us as we attempt to impact this world for Christ.

One final introductory thought to pastors, leaders, etc.: I am convinced God brought men to be discipled at our church because we had a passion for it. It is a most rewarding way to watch your church grow—and grow it will!

Go and be a Christian on a mission. It has great eternal rewards.

1

Our Story

THIS BOOK WAS WRITTEN with much prayer, concern, and fear that I might be misunderstood. Please read it and remember that I am still a work in progress and that I certainly do not have all the answers. I am writing from my own personal experience, hopeful it is the best way to help you see the big picture.

MY EARLY ADOLESCENCE

I grew up attending a quaint little county church that preached the gospel of Jesus Christ without apology. My family attended church faithfully. We were one of those families that when the church doors were open, you could count on us being there. How sad it is that this tradition is dying out today. It took a lot of preaching to fully prick my heart, although I may have been saved earlier and was just not clear on the truth. Maybe that is why Paul calls it the foolishness of preaching (1 Cor 1:21).

The Bible teaches that a person is born a sinner (Rom 5:12) and needs a Savior (Rom 5:17–19). Mankind will do all kinds of things to be their own savior. They will go to church, read the Bible, do good works, give money, try to keep the commandments, get baptized, and many other good and worthwhile things. Scripture is clear that man can neither save himself nor merit God's grace by his own actions (Eph 2:8–9). It is truly by grace that we are saved by our faith in Christ and Christ alone (Titus 3:5). Salvation is a free gift, and only by receiving this gift can one enter heaven. I understood this as a child, but it was not until a special week of preaching, called a revival, that I finally made this personal decision to accept Christ as my Savior. It was no longer my parents' faith. It was now clearly my faith. I wanted Jesus to forgive my sins. I wanted His forgiveness. I wanted to go to heaven. So, at the ripe old age of sixteen, I gave my life to Christ and waited for His call on my life. This is really where the story begins.

As God-centered as our little church was, and as God-centered as my family was, one thing was lacking: discipleship. As a sixteen-year-old adolescent with hormones bursting, long hair waiting, marijuana calling, rock music blaring, and a host of other things connected with the 1970s, I was a lone ship waiting for rocky bottoms. I didn't sin as badly as I could have, but I still drifted greatly, and it was not long before my zeal began to wane.

I saw an immediate change when Christ first came into my life (2 Cor 5:17). I wanted my friends to get saved. I wanted clear changes in my life. My love for church, the Lord, and other spiritual things truly exploded; however, my lack of personal discipleship training left me more like a loose wheel. I do not blame my family or local church for this lack of necessity. There is a worldwide neglect that has not improved during the last thirty years, and unfortunately, it is a very familiar story. I hear men say they are saved but not mature in their understanding of the Lord's commands, or they believe they are mature, when in reality they are not. American men often are self-driven, self-taught, self-motivated, and the church has left their maturity almost solely to them. This attitude is a sheer neglect of Matthew 28:18–20:

> And Jesus came and spake unto them, saying, All power is given unto me in heaven and in earth. Go ye therefore, and teach all nations, baptizing them in the name of the Father, and of the Son, and of the Holy Ghost: Teaching them to observe all things what-soever I have commanded you: and, lo, I am with you always, even unto the end of the world. Amen.

And Ephesians 4:11–16:

> And he gave some, apostles; and some, prophets; and some, evan-gelists; and some, pastors and teachers; For the perfecting of the saints, for the work of the ministry, for the edifying of the body of Christ: Till we all come in the unity of the faith, and of the knowl-edge of the Son of God, unto a perfect man, unto the measure of the stature of the fulness of Christ: That we henceforth be no more children, tossed to and fro, and carried about with every wind of doctrine by the sleight of men, and cunning craftiness, whereby they lie in wait to deceive; But speaking the truth in love, may grow up into him in all things, which is the head, even Christ:

> From whom the whole body fitly joined together and compacted by that which every joint supplieth, according to the effectual working in the measure of every part, maketh increase of the body unto the edifying of itself in love.

God has specifically given gifted men the responsibility to train up the church. To not do so is neglect, and it cannot be overlooked.

Now, let's get back to my personal journey. For the next two years of high school, my junior and senior years, I floundered. It seemed like I was taking two steps forward and three steps backward. There was no spiritual leader in my life who was taking an interest in my spiritual needs. I was trying to read the word, pray, and be faithful all on my own, but I was drifting. Nevertheless, God was still in my life, and it was only a matter of time before He stepped in to set things straight.

One side note to this journey is an unseen part to God's overall plan. I was blessed to have a praying mother and grandmother. I remember going to my grandparents' house, just two houses down the street from mine, on Saturday mornings to visit. We did not lock our doors back then, so I just opened their door and went in to visit. I often found my grandmother on her knees, with her face in a Bible, praying in ways that I could only imagine. She and my mother were regular pleaders with God for the family. No wonder that of the three sons born to my mother, two are pastors and one is a Christian school principal. Please never allow any program to exist without prayer.

ON TO BIBLE COLLEGE

During the summer of my junior year, my family came across the name of a Bible college. I was not really interested in going there. Although I had given my life to Christ, He was becoming an echo in the back of my mind. Inwardly I was dying spiritually and heading in the wrong direction. Plus, I was too interested in sports! I wanted to play college sports, and the local university was definitely my choice. I applied to both colleges, trying to appease my parents and hoping I would get to play sports. A funny thing happened in this process. My mother was the town postmaster. No mail came into our little town that did not pass my mother's hands. I am not accusing her of mail tampering, because that is a federal offense, however, I only heard back from the Bible college. After graduating from high school, I went to the only college that wanted me—or at least it was the only college that I was aware of that wanted me. I guess we will never know on this side of eternity, because my mother still denies it vehemently, and I am not sure it will matter on the other side. Whatever happened, it was truly the work of God. Maybe that is part of why I have embraced Philippians 1:6 as my life verse: "Being confident of this very thing, that he which hath begun a good work in you will perform it until the day of Jesus Christ."

There I was on the grounds of a Bible college. Saved by faith, but lost in sight, I had no idea what I was doing or where I was going. I remember the first night in my room with two other young men. One thought that it would be good to read some Scripture before we went to sleep. What a great idea! The suggestion was made that we read 1 John to begin, and I loved the idea, because I was trying to impress them. I began reading John 1. Obviously, any Bible scholar knows that 1 John and John 1 are two different chapters, but I had no clue.

Here I was, a believer for two years, and I did not know there was a book of the Bible called 1 John. I was truly lacking in knowledge. But God, who is rich in mercy, had another plan. The Bible college was perfect for me. It took a diamond in the rough and began to work on it ever so gently and graciously. God took me to be discipled, despite of the failure of the local church, and this is the core of this book. I am grateful for the Bible college and other para-church organizations that have come along and are still doing a great work for God. Their existence, however, does not relieve the local church from doing what it is called to do—to produce mature disciples. The Bible college came to my rescue, making me an exception to the rule. However, there is a better way.

TEACHING IN A CHRISTIAN HIGH SCHOOL

After Bible college, I taught at a Christian school. What a wonderful seven years of growth in my life. I was still single, so I had ample time to invest in the kids, the school, and the church. Nevertheless, there was something missing in my life and the church, or at least that is what I was thinking. I attended two different churches that were rather evangelical, and although one stressed evangelism and the other stressed Bible teaching, neither focused on discipleship in any way. I was still out there on my own regarding specific maturity and accountability. I think assumptions are made about men believing they are deeper spiritually than they really are.

It is part of the male ego to appear better than reality. Whereas women are more willing to open up, admit things, and seek help, men are more prone to believe they can do it on their own, which they rarely do. Egos feed their hard shell, keeping others at bay, especially those who might hold them accountable. Although I was maturing, there were still gaps in my life and instead of addressing those gaps, I began to assume this was just the way things were.

While teaching in the Christian school and becoming somewhat concerned about church, God was breaking my heart to go back to school and prepare for the pastorate. As I often thought maybe there was something lacking in the church, God would nudge me and suggest, "Why don't you do something about it?" It is always easier to complain, find fault, or criticize than it is to do something about the issue. It seemed God was saying to me, "Do something or shut up." Because my mouth rarely does the latter, it became evident that God was leading me to pastor in His field.

ON TO SEMINARY

I enrolled in seminary in the fall, and the tests were waiting for me as soon as I arrived on campus. The seminary had a Bible college at the same location, and I was offered teaching opportunities at the college while I attended seminary. Previously I had earned an M.A., so I was qualified to teach on the Bible college level. I also had two coaching opportunities waiting for me (baseball and basketball). I chose basketball, and as a result, I was able to fund my seminary training. Interestingly enough, I began to spend more and more time at the college. The need for teaching was increasing, and God was blessing my time in the classroom. Now I was entertaining the possibility of teaching on the Bible college level, but was this why God had sent me to seminary? I needed a reminder.

The summer before my last year at seminary, I received a call that the new president of the Bible college was cutting expenses and all part-time staff were being given their walking papers. The cut included me, and so a month before my last year of seminary was to begin, I wondered how I was going to be able to finish. Again, God had other plans. The previous summer I had been married, and because of the financial issues of a seminarian, I was able to move on the campus in a small efficiency. Needless to say, the cost was reasonable. Also, just days before we were to be in seminary, the Lord opened a door for me to work in the youth ministry in an inner-city church. What a rich reward this was for me. I was back in seminary with just a few classes to finish and wondering what the Lord had in store for me.

As the year progressed, it became obvious to me that Bible college was not my path. God quickly drew my heart back to the local church, and I began, once again, to revisit these possibilities. In January of my graduation year, I visited a professor friend's office and asked what his plans were for the future. He was looking to pastor and had just candidated at a church in the country that he planned to turn down. He mentioned it to me, and before long, I was preaching there for candidacy. In a few months, we were heading to the country for my first pastorate. I cannot explain how excited we were! We were expecting our first baby, going to live in a new parsonage, and heading to a church where the former pastor was in residence. This was the dream of a lifetime. I guess we can say that ignorance is bliss. I had no clue what I was getting into or what was awaiting me around the corner. I can say this; there was no first-year honeymoon. Nevertheless, we went in faith and trust, and God did not let us down.

FIRST PASTORATE

By summer, we were moved in and were ready for full-time ministry in a small, Bible-believing church. Our first board meetings were rather interesting. I did not know what to expect, because I had never been on a church board before. It was all new to me. The way the constitution of the church was established permitted an official board to consist of elders and deacons. The charter required a minimum of five men, but because the church was small, it was hard to find five elders. Therefore, my first board included the former pastor, two elders, and two deacons. When I arrived, one of the deacons stepped down so that the number remained at five.

I came to the elders' meetings with such enthusiasm, but it was not long before I realized that something was not right. There were several internal struggles that I had no knowledge of or preparation for. I was still of the old-school mindset of "Can't we just get along?" I realized quickly the answer was *no*. I remember one meeting at the parsonage where an elder and deacon were late, with no call to let us know they would be late. When they arrived, I mentioned their tardiness and was basically told that I should have been thankful they even came. At one board meeting, the former pastor and one of the elders had a rather heated argument. As the new kid on the block, I discovered I had to grow up fast.

After a few months, I began having Bible studies on Saturday mornings for the men. Soon ten or so men were in attendance with some regularity. This was truly the birthing room for what this book is all about. The men came hungry. Although we had Sunday school, Sunday morning worship, Sunday night services, and Wednesday prayer meeting, the men were asking for more. Now I was only one person with a weak church board and a fast-growing church, and I was in way over my head. I did all the preaching and teaching (except Sunday school), made all the visits, led all the meetings, and was trying to be a new father. Sleep was just not happening.

LOOKING FOR HELP

I then realized what the church was missing—gray-haired men. I started praying that God would send me gray-haired men who could help me lead this ministry and as the old saying goes, be careful what you pray for, because you just might get it.

The church graciously ordained me rather early, and I was on my way as a pastor of a Bible-believing church. The ordination, a major requirement to pastor, was a key ingredient to what was to lie ahead. I did not recognize it at the time, but the message by one of my seminary professors, Dr. George Harton of Capital Bible Seminary, became very instrumental in the future of this church. It truly laid an incredible foundation. He preached on 2 Timothy 2:2, which says, "And the things that thou hast heard of me among many witnesses, the same commit thou to faithful men, who shall be able to teach others also." This challenged me to train up men to take on the ministry. I had heard that passage before, and after college and seminary, I could actually find 2 Timothy without the tabs. I heard the message, but it still was not registering in my heart. Nevertheless, *I* clearly had a plan. *I* was teaching men on Saturday morning and praying for gray-haired men. It was only a matter of time before this church was going to be a happening place, or so *I* thought.

Also during this time, God sent a fellow pastor into my life who was going to be a major player in the whole process. He was pastoring at a nearby church, and he quickly took me under his wing. Although he only had small amounts of time to give me, Pastor Rick Leinweber was extremely valuable. He gave me many materials and supplies. I owe much to his gracious support. I began to read, study, pray, and observe more than ever. Seminary was extremely valuable, and I would recommend to anyone entering the ministry to attend seminary. However, seminary is not a replacement for on-the-job training. I went from boot camp to the front lines, and I was not ready. Again, I am not blaming anyone in particular, but the one thing that was consistently missing in my training was one-on-one discipleship. No one had ever taken time to help me mature my walk.

Let's go back to my prayer requests for gray-haired men. During the next several years, I kept the Saturday-morning Bible study going, and God truly sent me two gray-haired men. It was not long before they were both elders with me, giving us an entire elder board of five elders. Now *my* plan was working as established, or so *I* thought.

Without going into all the details, the two gray-haired men did not work out very well. I now had a bigger problem than at the start. There were more conflicts, more division, and more issues than ever before. And the church was bursting at the seams. I remember many times just putting my hands over my face and wondering why I got involved in church ministry. What was I thinking? Then I remembered that I did not volunteer. This was the Lord's army, and I was drafted (1 Cor 1:26). There was no room for being AWOL. There was no jumping ship. God called, and He would have to see me through. I have learned there is no challenge too great for my God. The Christian journey often is very hard, but it is right. When you understand God's call on your life, you do not debate the circumstances. You surrender your will to His leading and trust Him for the future. Life is not about us. This is His story (history), and we are to live it out in His perspective.

On one of those days when I had my face in my hands, my mind was brought back to my seminary professor's message at my ordination service. It was as if the message was being preached to me a second time in its entirety. There I sat in my office contemplating what to do, and the message several years earlier was ringing loud and clear. It was God speaking in His so gentle and clear way, "Why not train leaders up yourself?" What a novel idea . . . *not!* It is greatly detailed in Scripture, modeled by the Savior, and commanded for the church. Because I often am slow to get it, God had to teach this to me in college, seminary, at the ordination, and then bring me to a place of despair before I finally got it. Many who are reading this must think I am a slow learner. You are absolutely right in this case, but once I did get it, I understood. The only question left was how to begin.

THE BIRTH OF MEN WITH A MISSION

After prayer and research, I decided to start a men's ministry with the specific design of training men to be mature in Christ. Second Timothy 2:2, "And the things that thou hast heard of me among many witnesses, the same commit thou to faithful men, who shall be able to teach others also," became my theme verse, and off I went to develop the material. Because of the uniqueness of what I was doing, I did not seek help about how to develop a men's ministry. I wanted this to be the Lord's and mine.

I began by asking twelve men (the spiritual number) to join me on a journey. I personally picked men from the church who had shown some desire and love for the Lord. We began to meet one Monday night per month. Because the church was still growing and I was heavily involved in many other things, the material often was being prepared right up to class time. I used my files extensively and mass copied material for them to study. The first night I just taught a lesson, gave my vision to them, and assigned a study for them to be prepared for the next month's study. There seemed to be an excitement brewing, but I had no idea. I was really flying by the seat of my pants, and these pants were getting worn thin. The men were returning, studying, and memorizing the verses, and the journey was developing. God had instilled a hunger, and to Him must be the glory.

We met that first year for nine Mondays from September to May. I gave them the summer off for numerous reasons, mostly because I was out of material. We had studied themes such as prayer, Bible study, evangelism, discipleship, and other related themes that I thought men would enjoy. They did, but I wondered where to go next. Plus, another problem was developing. New men who did not get in on the first class, either because I did not ask them to be a part or because they had come to the church after we began (once the class started, I was not allowing folks to come in midstream), were asking to be a part of the class. God was stirring the hearts of the men to want to be a part of this ministry.

It seems clear to me that God will send men to you if you have a channel for them to mature. Maybe the reason God does not give some churches men who want to grow is because they would not grow at that church. If God is the Great Architect of His church (which He is), and if God sets us in the body as He sees fit (which He does), then maybe He also orchestrates moves, transfers, and gives hunger as well. Once the program was in place in our church, men were coming from all over. There was no publicity, but the Holy Spirit was bringing them in. What was I to do? I did not want the classes combined, because I felt there was some cohesiveness with the first group. So we began a second year to coincide with the first one. I also gave names to these classes so they could be distinguished. Thus, the name *Men with a Mission* was coined, and to keep the years separate, we called them, rather ingeniously, *Men with a Mission 1* and *Men with a Mission 2.* What insight!

I had two classes on Monday nights two weeks apart with about the same agenda. I was giving assignments, memory verses, reading of Scripture, and other related themes. But I was noticing another problem; one night a month was not enough for the men. They desired more time, more study material, and more research projects. I can truly say that a hunger was developing. Someone once said that the way to get rid of your pastor is to hunger for the word of God in such a way that he will kill himself trying to feed you. There might be some truth to that. I often hear there is no hunger for the truth among God's people, and I challenge this thought. I believe the hunger is there, and you need to cultivate it in your people. You cannot give your people a steady diet of TV clips, news articles, etc., and expect their hunger for God's word to grow. Along with the problem of the men in the church wanting more, and the church continuing to grow, I was still a lone ranger with a few elders and staff, and there were more men wanting to join the class.

It might be important to note that Promise Keepers was just getting started at this time. I am convinced that Promise Keepers struck a nerve within the men in the body of Christ simply because the church was not doing the work she was called to do—namely, training up the men. Men were hungering for more than a sermonette on Sunday mornings and a few other times of study. Men were looking for the deep things of God, but it was nowhere to be found. Along came Promise Keepers and the challenges from many great teachers. Men flocked to it, accepted the challenge, and were fired up. I have seen over the years that men's schedules will get filled. The question is, "What is going to fill it?" Little League, work, golf, fishing, hunting, or whatever, men are going to have full schedules. I decided that I wanted to call for their time and invest in them spiritual truths that would help change their lives and better their families. They accepted the call.

We were now entering the third year, and there were going to be three different classes. Some of the earlier men had dropped out because of the difficulty of memorization, or reading, but we were moving on with the rest. To keep the challenge high and the groups different, I decided to call year three Eldership Training. The big picture was becoming clearer. I was in need of elders, and there were none to be found; elder-type men were not just dropping in and asking to be an elder, so something had to be done. The class needed to be training elders. I found material directly connected with eldership, and off we went into year three. Since I still had not discovered the answer for the need for more nights for the men, the third year I taught three different groups of men: *Men with a Mission 1, Men with a Mission 2,* and *Eldership Training* on three consecutive Mondays, and for three years.

A SUMMER EVALUATION

I was only planning to offer three years. Hey, Jesus had only three years with His men, right? Plus, I was clearly out of material. However, it was obvious the hunger was not dissipating. The following summer, I took the entire months of June and July off to develop the men's manuals, think through the future of the class, and prepare for whatever the Lord had in mind. I believe it is always best to discover God's plan and join His work, instead of asking Him to bless our work. This had been His work from the beginning, because I really had no clue what I was doing. He had been faithful. I just needed to trust Him for what was to come.

That summer God gave me the material for three manuals, which are available in print, DVD, and PowerPoint, as a supplement to this book.[1]

With the manuals, I decided there needed to be some adjustments. We combined the first two years and kept the third year separate. All three years were titled *Men with a Mission,* designated by year. We had to drop the word "elder" out of the training because some men assumed they would be elders after the class. I was still learning. Each class met

---

1. There are many individuals who helped put this into the present form, since I am technologically challenged. These folks were mentioned in the preface. I am grateful to the many men and women who have made this program a blessing.

twice per month. Each class had memory verses. Each class was required to have a prayer partner, a ministry, and to be committed to the program fully. All work had to be completed to proceed to the next year. All verses had to be memorized to proceed to the next year. And only the first year was open to the church at large. After the first year, one had to be a member of our local church.

I realize that some may find fault here. Please let me explain our reasoning. God had called me to pastor a local church to which I personally felt and assumed enormous responsibility. These were the folks to whom I was called to minister. These were the folks I prayed for, visited, challenged, and worked with regularly. God had not called me to do this for other churches, because I was only one person. Plus, I did not want to cause any hard feelings with other pastors who might think I was trying to steal their sheep. I had enough of my own problems and was not interested in theirs. Membership causes the individual to make a serious commitment to study beyond the general callousness of church and be an active member of a vibrant local church. I do not believe any ministry, program, or organization can function to its fullest without the local church. In the Old Testament, God worked through Israel to bless the world. Now He is working through the church. To have any program or ministry that is disconnected from the local church is unwise and unbiblical. I pressed the men to be committed and make Men with a Mission the supplement, not the full agenda.

There are several more ingredients that need to be explained. Since the men were completing an intentional three-year program, we decided to offer a graduation. During the summer after their third year, we offered a class graduation with diplomas, gifts, and a special night of dinner and the works. All graduates from previous years are also invited every year, so the group continues to grow. On the program we list the graduates and their ministries. These graduates, over the years, are fulfilling all the key positions in our church. There is not a key position, such as elder, deacon, or ministry leader, that is not filled by a graduate of Men with a Mission. As a matter of fact, it has now become a requirement for any position. We will not even consider a man for a position in the church who is not taking the class. This has provided us with men who have been trained to handle Scripture, have convictions, and have accountability. By the way, two of the men who were in that very first class with me are now elders in the church, one of whom is on the pastoral staff.

With my limited vision, I was unable to see what was coming ahead. Men began to ask for more. I was unable to provide anything else, so they began to look elsewhere—Bible colleges, graduate schools, and other places—to learn. The class has instilled a hunger in the men that was not to be quenched. Since then, we have had men attend Bible college, graduate schools, online studies, and other types of learning. It seems as if they cannot get enough. And what is even more exciting is that these men are sharing with our people as they are learning. The adult Sunday school classes are actual forums to convey learning that is going on all over the church. This is another blessing I was unable to see at the time. Our whole church is reaping the benefit of this discipleship ministry.

Not all men were able to go to college, etc. Therefore, we began another program called Reading with a Mission. We would allow any graduate who wanted to be involved in this reading program, and many did. These were books I had read or was reading, and we would offer a book every several months to the men. If they read the book and came to a Saturday-morning discussion, the book was free, a gift from the church. If they failed to read the book or attend the class, they had to pay for the book. We did this for several years, and it has been rather successful.

ANOTHER ADDITION

This past year we launched Men with a Mission 4. It was a pilot year for the graduates, and after making a few blunders, we believe we understand what is best for this class. We began with doctrinal studies. The first was Christology. They had to research it in stages, write a paper based on their research, and memorize Scripture. We tackled memorizing the entire book of Philippians, and at least half of the class finished this memory work. Yet, because the topic and research skills were still lacking, I needed to be more specific and detailed. So we purchased Systematic Theology textbooks and will study them in the year to come. So far we meet only once per month for the fourth year. These men are heavily involved in ministry. We do not want to overwhelm them, although we still want to challenge them. We also believe it is critical to nail down every man's theology in an era of weak theology, which the church overall is experiencing. We believe right belief will help dictate right behavior.

Now the class was selling itself to the church. Men were pursuing men who had not attended and drawing them into the class. We made one more adjustment to our attendance policy. I still sent out a letter to several men personally inviting them, but now we also put the class in the bulletin as a general offering. We wanted no man to be left behind. On an information night in August before the class began, we invited all who might be interested in joining. We went over the class and asked them to pray about being a part of it. They had several weeks to do so, and if they did, they were to commit for one year at a time. They had to attend all classes, seventeen per year. They were allowed two misses before they would have to repeat the year. I have found that men need the boundaries. They also had to memorize all the verses, approximately fifty per year. As amazing as this may sound, I have found that every man who has taken the class has been able to do the memory work. We have convinced adults that memorizing Scripture is too hard. Shame on us! There needs to be a concerted effort to get believers to hide God's word in their hearts; it is essential.

At the beginning of each class, every man has a chance to recite his Scripture memory to the class. Each man has to recite at least one passage. They also have a three-by-five-inch card that I hand out every week with the numbers one through seventeen on it. On the corresponding night, they mark whether they had finished their lesson and did their memory work. This helps with accountability, although it is purely an honor system. At the end of the night, which usually lasts about two hours, the men break off with their accountability partner for prayer. Each man has a partner in the class. The third-year class also has a first-year man on his prayer sheet and someone he will check in with periodically to make sure he is keeping up. We also added three more men to the leadership of Men with a Mission. Although I still, as the senior pastor, do most of the teaching, I have one graduate assigned to accountability for the men, one man assigned to help with Scripture memory, and one man to substitute. Actually, all three men are able teachers and fill in for me periodically.

It is probably fitting at this time to mention a few comments from the wives about this class. One woman told her husband that it should be called Men with a Secret. I am not sure exactly why, because we did not want this class to be a secret. As a matter of fact, one of the requirements was for the men to recite the Scriptures to their wives. We want the ladies involved in this as well. We want the men to begin to disciple at home. In addition, many wives have come up to me and said things like, "I don't know what you have done with my husband in that class, but I like it."

Many wives have encouraged their husbands, supported their husbands, and helped in the process because they have seen a change in their men. I have never met a Christian lady yet who did not want her husband to deepen his walk with God. Our ladies do not see this as a threat in any way. They are our biggest supporters.

As we close this section of our study, I want to make it clear this is all about grace. That God would choose to use me is an amazing story. Believe me when I say, if God can use me, He can use anyone willing to make him or herself available. He can use you. Our story is not about us. It is about an amazing God who can do amazing things. Keep on reading, and prepare to be a disciple-maker for the Great Disciple-Maker and watch Him work.

2

Old Testament Mandate

In my first year of Men with a Mission, my class was asked two critical questions. "How many of you feel qualified to teach someone else?" No one raised a hand. "How many of you know more about the Bible than a brand-new Christian?" Everyone raised their hand. "Then you're qualified to teach someone else." My head was spinning. How could I—a twenty-five-year-old man—teach someone else the word of God? It didn't matter; the point was clear. So I started a Bible study in my home with two men who were younger in the Lord than I. After some time, I began more Bible studies with other families. That grew into teaching children in Sunday school. God continued to challenge me in many areas of my life; I became an elder and began teaching adults in Sunday school. The next step was Bible college, and today I'm an associate pastor, leading and feeding sheep on a full-time basis. That one statement changed my entire life: "Then you're qualified to teach someone else."

—Personal testimony of Marvin R. Patrick
Associate Pastor, Mount Airy Bible Church

ALTHOUGH JESUS WAS THE master disciple-maker, the concept is detailed in the Old Testament. It seems that almost every key leader believed it was necessary to invest in a younger apprentice to carry on his ministry and message for God after he was gone. In the early chapters of the Old Testament, discipling was primarily a father-son concept, and understandably so, because that is the foundation of the Old Testament. It would take years before the one family of Abraham would be a mighty nation. Until that time occurred, there was the necessity of one man to carry the message to another for the communication of God's entire message, which we have today called the Bible.

Before Genesis 12, there are four major events, which cover those eleven chapters. First is creation, which covers primarily Genesis 1–2. Adam leads mankind into sin, the second major event, and this is detailed for us in Genesis 3, with some history overlap in Genesis 4–5. The worldwide flood is the third major event detailed for us in Genesis 6–10. The fourth major event, the Tower of Babel, is detailed in chapter 11. Humanity was greatly increasing, but after the flood, there were only eight people remaining on the Earth: Noah's family, who survived in the Ark. We know little of the details of Noah and how he communicated information about God and life to his family, but we can be assured that he did. Yet, it is not until Genesis 12 where this idea of personal discipleship really develops.

ABRAHAM AS A DISCIPLE-MAKER

In Genesis 12, God calls a man named Abram (actually, the exact call comes at the end of chapter 11) to leave his family and become a great nation. He promises Abram he is going to have a family that is going to bless the world. He also will have posterity that will be as innumerable as the stars of the sky and the sand of the oceans. He was going to make Abram a great nation. Because of this call, Abram put his faith in God to do exactly as God said He would do.

Hebrews 11 describes this man's faith for us. God did not tell Abram the exact details about how everything would fall into place; however, you can be sure that Abram knew the importance of passing all that he knew and discovered on to his sons, and their sons, and for them to pass it on to their sons. Although not explained, such a progression can be discovered by examining the faith of his family. Hebrews 11 mentions by name Abram's son, Isaac, his grandson, Jacob, and his great-grandson, Joseph, as models of the faith that Abram possessed. God did give direct revelation to each of these men, but you have to believe that the faith of Abram was being passed on to generation after generation. How else would they have known? One such example is the "sacrifice" of Isaac, which we will examine more closely later.

Abram seems to take seriously his faith and the giving of his faith to his sons, and before Abram has any children, he takes responsibility for his nephew, Lot. If we only had the Old Testament to examine, we would probably conclude that Abram's discipleship of Lot was an utter failure. Yet the New Testament clearly calls Lot a righteous man (2 Pet 2:7). When did Lot develop this kind of faith to be called righteous? The only man in his life to have had such righteousness was his uncle, Abram (later called Abraham).

Romans 4:9 mentions that Abraham believed God, and it was accounted to him for righteousness (the same root word to describe "just" Lot in 2 Peter 2). Where did Lot learn of righteousness? The obvious answer is from his righteous uncle, Abraham. And if you follow this righteous Abraham in Genesis, you will discover a true man of faith who modeled it for his nephew. In Genesis 12:8, he modeled worship and sacrifice for Lot. In Genesis 13, he modeled unselfishness when he gave Lot the choice of land and took the land that remained. In Genesis 14, he modeled faith as he took on a large army to rescue Lot from those who had captured him.

There is no question that Lot learned of righteousness by the example of Abraham. Abraham was investing in the next generation. There is probably much more that could be said about what Abraham specifically taught Lot, but we do not have biblical records for support. We would have to read into some passages, but I am not sure from the whole of what is recorded that it would be too far from the actual truth. For the New Testament to call him "righteous Lot," there has to have been more influence and teaching than what is recorded. The point is that Abraham caught the vision and mandate from God early: invest in others.

Eventually, Abraham has a son named Isaac. Isaac is described in the New Testament as a man of faith in Hebrews 11. Where did he learn of the faith necessary to please God? I believe the answer lies with his father. Abraham is personalizing his faith, but he also is propagating his faith. And because the Hebrews were to remain distinct from the world, Abraham's biggest investment would have been in his family. Isaac certainly carries on the faith of his father. The prominent episode where this faith was strengthened probably occurred when Isaac laid on the altar in Genesis 22. Genesis 22:8 reveals such a faith when Abraham said to Isaac that God would provide a ram for the sacrifice. He was practicing his faith, and Isaac clearly accepted this faith. But it does not end with his family.

In Genesis 25, Isaac and Rebekah have twins, Esau and Jacob. Jacob practiced the faith of his father, as the New Testament verifies. Abraham's faith was traveling from generation to generation, and the concept of passing on that which we have learned was becoming the general practice. In the Old Testament, God was continuing to reveal just who He was to each generation. His names were revealed in each situation and circumstance. Although God may have revealed Himself in ways the Old Testament does not explain, it can be assumed that each generation knew certain things about God because they were told those things. Discipleship of the attributes and character of God was truly happening in the Old Testament, as each patriarch passed it down one person at a time.

So far, we have only seen this modeled in the family. Abraham modeled it to his son Isaac and nephew, Lot, and Isaac to his son Jacob, and we could certainly discuss the faith of Joseph, the son of Jacob. Abraham understood the necessity of passing his faith along for his posterity, and they accepted the same challenge. By the end of Genesis, this family was seventy strong, and their faith was clearly substantive. It was present enough that they grasped major truths about God, including the need to separate, have only one God, fear Him, and understand their call to be His people. These cannot be taken lightly. Discipleship was in the early stages of development.

MOSES AS A DISCIPLE-MAKER

At the beginning of Exodus, Moses is the central figure. Moses is not in the direct family line of Abraham, but he is of the overall family tree. He is a descendent of Abraham, and he had the same faith as Abraham more than five hundred years later. It was clear that the plan was working. Abraham has greatly distributed his faith to his descendents. Imagine that the faith of this one man propagated itself to several million people—the number of Israel at the beginning of Exodus. I believe Abraham was an incredible discipler and communicator of the truths of God. Moses picks up the call and leads the entire nation in this faith. He even gets the distinct privilege of being on Mount Sinai to receive the Law from God and the details of how to live out this life of faith. Moses also understood the importance of having a prodigy. For the next forty years, he carefully takes with him the man who will become the next in line to lead this great nation: Joshua.

Moses and Joshua may be the best examples of a disciple in the entire Old Testament. Moses received his call clearly from God. Exodus 3 describes for us a unique encounter as Moses hears directly from God via the burning bush. God begins with a short introduction of Himself as He explains that He is, "The God of thy father, the God of Abraham, the God of Isaac, and the God of Jacob" (Exod 3:6a). This is a record that is brought to the attention of Moses about how he received this faith. Moses was a believer as a result of the incredible work of the patriarchs ahead of him. Because they had embraced the faith and passed it on, he enjoyed the fruit of their labors and had the responsibility placed in his lap. In other words, would there be faithful followers after Moses?

We have the record of proof, but in that precise moment, Moses was faced with the responsibility of keeping the faith or passing along the faith. Remember, there were no written Scriptures for others to come into the faith, and this was God's only plan. The Jews were to pass it on. Of course we understand God's sovereignty, but in a sense, the success of this plan was in the hands of Moses. What would he do with this information about God? God could have sent a memo to all the people. He could have provided a book. Instead, He called one man to do this task. Moses was that man. Exodus 3 explains this clearly. Exodus 3:9 mentions that God heard the cry of His people. Their cry came up to Him resoundingly. But Exodus 3:10 says God was coming to Moses to send him. God's plan could not have been clearer. If God's people were going to get the truths of God, they were going to get it via a messenger, and he was to pass it on.

In the same chapter, God promises victory in this journey (v. 20) and lays out for Moses the correct path. It is as if God said, "Go to the elders and enlist them in this plan and watch me work a work that will amaze even Pharaoh." The people would even be given jewels to help with their travels. God had the entire work all planned, but He did so through a leader. It was up to the leader to ensure the message and plan were carried out.

In chapter 4, God appointed Aaron to assist Moses. There is debate about whether this was God's ideal or just a way to enable Moses to go forth. Moses was full of objections about being God's man, and Aaron was to assist Moses to complete the job. Yet it was clear that Aaron would not be Moses's successor. Moses would have to develop another man to ensure that when Moses could no longer lead, the mission was still in place and moving forward.

By Exodus 17, Moses has seen much of the hand of God at work. Remember that Moses was still learning about God. We do not know how much of the knowledge of God was given to him via his mother and in the days of his weaning, but that may have been a short amount of time. Moses spent much of his early years in the courts of Pharaoh—not exactly a hot-bed of theologically sound knowledge. The next forty years of his life were spent with his father-in-law in Midian in the wilderness as a shepherd. I am not convinced that his father-in-law was a theologian of any sort. He is called a priest of Midian, and there is no evidence to believe this is a priest of God's order. He does not show any theological insight about God; so again, Moses is not getting a lot of information about God from here.

Moses, because of some lapses in the patriarchal line in true disciple-making, was limited to the scope of God. God's people were drifting, and God was personally writing for them what He expected and who He really was. Moses would be the only messenger to receive God's law and make sure that it was given to the people. There would not be two million copies of the Law. God's plan was to have one Law, one set of tablets, and one leader. Moses was needed to ensure that God's word ended up in the minds of God's people. Moses was to pass it on. Moses was also wise enough to know that he could not do this forever, and he could not do this alone. This was a task far beyond his ability and skill. When he looked for a man he could invest his life and the mission into, he found Joshua.

In Exodus 17, Moses was faced once again with the difficulty of leading these people. What was he to do with such a rebellious people? God told him in Exodus 17:5 to stand before the people with the elders—already a hint to plurality of leadership—and speak with the people. He does so, and right after this, Amalek, a foreign enemy, comes in and fights against Israel. Exodus 17:9 says, "And Moses said unto Joshua, Choose us out men, and go out, fight with Amalek: to morrow I will stand on the top of the hill with the rod of God in mine hand." Who is Joshua? Where did he come from? We can only speculate, but it is clear from this important task, and others that follow, that Moses saw something in Joshua. What was it? Maybe he saw the potential and was willing to invest the time.

It was clear Joshua would take the lead and find men to fight with him. Joshua was given a major task. First, he would be responsible for finding the right kind of men to go with him. Second, he would be responsible to destroy this enemy. Israel was stalled in the trenches and could not move forward. This was a major resistance to their cause and direction, and should Joshua fail, Israel would not be able to go forward. Moses had to have known the gravity of such a request. To put this assignment in any person's hands would not have been acceptable. This was of the utmost importance. Joshua was the man.

In many senses of the word, Moses spent the rest of his life training Joshua for the task that followed—take Israel into the land and pass the faith along. Moses did it masterfully. Of all the things that Moses is credited for, this might be the least mentioned. However, in terms of God's plan, it is one of the most important. The future of God's plan, although it ultimately lies with God, from an earthly perspective, lies with mankind. Joshua was trained and became that man. The result of Moses's choice of Joshua on this first assignment was critical. He proved faithful. Moses had a man to follow him, and God received all the glory. As Exodus 17 closes, Moses builds an altar and calls it Jehovah-nissi, meaning, "The Lord is my Banner." A banner is a statement about something specific. In this case, God was making a statement that the birth of the nation, begun years ago via Abraham, was now to make great strides on the path promised by God. Israel was to become a nation to be noticed and respected from that day forward.

Other situations in which Moses used Joshua deserve emphasis. Exodus 24 records when Moses ascended Mount Sinai. In verse 12, the Lord calls Moses up to the mount. Verse 13 says Moses "rose up, and his minister, Joshua." It is implied that Joshua knew to go with him. The ground was being laid for Joshua to take over. Verse 14 makes it clear that Moses took Joshua with him. Although Moses is, and should be, credited with the gathering of the law, it should not be overlooked that Joshua was part of that process. God was grooming the man to take Moses's place.

In Exodus 33:11, we are able to see into the heart of this one chosen to follow Moses. Joshua is described as one who "departed not out of the tabernacle." We know it does not mean he slept and ate there, because this would not be possible. What it means is Joshua understood it was necessary to prepare his heart. Moses could only do so much for Joshua. Joshua had to be drawing near to the heart of God as well.

The book of Leviticus does not mention Joshua. It is important to recognize this book is about their worship. The Israelites do not travel during this book and are probably still at Mount Sinai. Joshua does not need to be included in this book, and there is no attempt to make any connection between Moses and Joshua.

In Numbers, Joshua reappears. A scene of the lives of two men in Numbers 11:26–30 begins to reveal the loyalty of the man Joshua. Two men, Eldad and Medad, begin to prophesy and are, in a way, diverting attention from Moses. Joshua does not take this lightly. He goes to Moses and requests they be stopped. Joshua knows Moses is the leader, and he wants to be sure nothing is done to distract from his leadership. Good leaders understand and respect authority. Joshua believed they were circumventing Moses's leadership and desired to put an end to it. Moses would have none of it. Moses not only modeled humility before his follower, but he also encouraged Joshua to see the big picture. Leadership is never about a man or his following; it is always about the Lord and His leading.

Numbers 13 describes one of the more prominent times that Joshua surfaces in the Old Testament outside of the book of Joshua. It is in this chapter that the twelve spies are sent into the promised land to evaluate the land and determine a strategy. God told Moses to send men, one from each tribe, to view the land, and one of the twelve was Joshua (Num 13:8). This passage does reveal it was Moses who changed Joshua's name. Numbers 13:16 says, "Moses called Oshea the son of Nun Jehoshua." Apparently Hoshea was the name he was born with and declared by his birth parents, but it is Moses who changes his name to Joshua. Hoshea means "salvation," but Joshua means "Yahweh saves." The latter form is the Hebrew spelling for "Jesus." Moses was developing this new leader well.

Numbers 14 describes the response of the people from the exact action of the calling in chapter 13. Joshua and eleven other men entered the promised land from Kadesh Barnea and gave a mixed report. Joshua and Caleb were ready to take the land, which Caleb reported in chapter 13. Joshua was interestingly quiet. Yet, he was not quiet in chapter 14. He and Caleb spoke out; however, notice that Joshua was mentioned first. Read carefully these words in their entirety:

> And Joshua the son of Nun, and Caleb the son of Jephunneh, which were of them that searched the land, rent their clothes: And they spake unto all the company of the children of Israel, saying, The land, which we passed through to search it, is an exceeding good land. If the LORD delight in us, then he will bring us into this land, and give it us; a land which floweth with milk and honey. Only rebel not ye against the LORD, neither fear ye the people of the land; for they are bread for us: their defence is departed from them, and the LORD is with us: fear them not. But all the congregation bade stone them with stones. And the glory of the LORD appeared in the tabernacle of the congregation before all the children of Israel (Num 14:6–10).

Joshua clearly took the lead and is calling the people to go forward. We know they did not, and the loss was immense. Joshua was capable of leading in knowledge, but the people were not ready to follow him. Moses had more work to complete.

Joshua "disappears" for the next twelve chapters, and when he resurfaces again in chapter 27, Moses is prepared to name Joshua as the next leader of Israel. It is again necessary to record this section at length to get the full picture:

> And Moses spake unto the LORD, saying, Let the LORD, the God of the spirits of all flesh, set a man over the congregation, Which may go out before them, and which may go in before them, and which may lead them out, and which may bring them in; that the congregation of the LORD be not as sheep which have no shepherd. And the LORD said unto Moses, Take thee Joshua the son of Nun, a man in whom is the spirit, and lay thine hand upon him; and set him before Eleazar the priest, and before all the congregation; and give him a charge in their sight. And thou shalt put some of thine honour upon him, that all the congregation of the children of Israel may be obedient. And he shall stand before Eleazar the priest, who shall ask counsel for him after the judgment of Urim before the LORD: at his word shall they go out, and at his word they shall come in, both he, and all the children of Israel with him, even all the congregation. And Moses did as the LORD commanded him: and he took Joshua, and set him before Eleazar the priest, and before all the congregation: And he laid his hands upon him, and gave him a charge, as the LORD commanded by the hand of Moses (Num 27:15–23).

There are several important truths to be recognized. First, it was God who told Moses it was time to do so. Second, this confirmation was to take place publicly. Joshua was to be brought before the people and Eleazar. Third, Moses was to put some of his honor on Joshua. This made it clear to all the people that Moses recognized Joshua as the man to take his place. Fourth, Moses was to tell the people they were to obey Joshua's leadership, just as they had done for him. It was now set in stone: Moses had prepared Joshua to take his place, and the time was near at hand. Numbers 32:12 further confirmed why Joshua was God's choice, for he "wholly followed the Lord." It is hard not to confirm someone with this going for him.

Deuteronomy includes one specific reference that again suggests the idea that we are to duplicate ourselves in the ministry, because the work of the Lord is always bigger than one man.

> And I spake unto you at that time, saying, I am not able to bear you myself alone: The LORD your God has multiplied you, and, behold, ye are this day as the stars of heaven for multitude. (The LORD God of your fathers make you a thousand times so many more than you are, and bless you, as he hath promised you!) How can I myself alone bear your cumbrance, and your burden, and your strife? Take you wise men, and understanding, and known among your tribes, and I will make them rulers over you. And ye answered me, and said, The thing which thou hast spoken is good for us to do. So I took the chief of your tribes, wise men, and known, and made them heads over you, captains over thousands, and captains over hundreds, and captains over fifties, and captains over tens, and officers among your tribes (Deut 1:9–15).

One may argue this is more of a political endeavor than a spiritual one, and in some sense this would be correct. The overall point is that the calling is too big, and we cannot bear it alone. So it is with the call of the church. We are to develop leaders to help with the ministry and also to take over the ministry. None of us know the length of time we have to invest in the lives of those around us. We need to make the days and hours count for eternity. Joshua was not included in this group because he was discipled for an entirely different reason than these men.

Deuteronomy is primarily a review of the Law. All those who were twenty years and older who had first heard the Law had died in these wilderness wanderings. A review of the Law for this new generation was needed. There is not much movement between Joshua and Moses during this book. Deuteronomy 1:38 mentions that Joshua stood before Moses. Deuteronomy 3:21 is merely a review of earlier victories Joshua had observed. Deuteronomy 31:7–8 is a review of the call upon Joshua by Moses and of course, the Lord. Once again Moses reminds Joshua of his ancestry. "This has been passed down to you, Joshua. Do not let it die with you." Deuteronomy 31:23 records the charge that Moses gave to Joshua. Deuteronomy 34:9 proves that Moses had done his work well. The verse reads as follows, "And Joshua the son of Nun was full of the spirit of wisdom; for Moses had laid his hands upon him. And the children of Israel hearkened unto him, and did as the Lord commanded Moses." I suggest the hand upon Joshua was more than just some public ceremony. Moses had put his life on Joshua, and Joshua was ready to go forward.

Moses dies and God buries him, and Joshua takes over. It is clear from Joshua 1 that Joshua has truly listened to his mentor. Moses told him to be "strong and of a good courage," and now he was communicating the same words to his followers. Moses had truly prepared Joshua well. Moses had led Israel out of Egypt. Moses had led them to the promised land. Moses had received and communicated the Law to the people. Moses had been a great leader. I believe, however, his investment in Joshua will go down as one of his greatest feats, if not the greatest. One verse sums up well the great work Moses did with Joshua, "On that day the LORD magnified Joshua in the sight of all Israel; and they feared him, as they feared Moses, all the days of his life" (Josh 4:14).

JOSHUA AS A DISCIPLE-MAKER

Joshua takes over after Moses; he does a work of excellence in leading Israel into the land and settling it. He must have communicated the Law as well, as you see on several occurrences the people's understanding of the Law. They were now in the land and ready to be the people called by God to Abraham some six hundred years ago. The God of Abraham, Isaac, Jacob, and Moses was now the God of Joshua. The word had been passed down completely. It was time to go forward. Disciple-making had arrived.

No other time in Jewish history was there as much doubt as there was before Joshua. The people were not in their land, the revelation of God was only passed on orally, and there was no leader in view for the people. There was even a sense of remaining forever in Egypt. Moses became the man to take the people to the next level. He did so with forty years of faithful work and by passing the torch on to Joshua. The years these two men covered were some of the most critical years in all of Israel's history. If Moses failed, the plan was in great jeopardy. He did not fail, and today we are still enjoying the fruits of his labors. He did so with timely investment in the life of one man. I am not sure that it is possible to fully grasp the importance of this work. There is only one other time recorded in history where this work was of equal importance. It was with our Savior and His investment in the twelve disciples. We will review this key time later in our study. I believe we are living in a similar time as they experienced and that we also need to view this investment as critical. Hopefully my passion, which is fully founded in Scripture, will urge your hearts to make 2 Timothy 2:2 the mission of your church.

Let's get back to our Old Testament study. As much as I am convinced Moses fully grasped this passion and passed it on to Joshua in a personal way, I am not sure Joshua understood his responsibility. Joshua appears to take more of a lone ranger approach to leadership and when he dies, the time period of the Judges begins, which clearly appears to be devoid of God. Joshua did not pass it on well, as verified in Judges 2:10, "And also all that generation were gathered unto their fathers; and there arose another generation after them, which knew not the LORD, nor yet the works which he had done for Israel." The time of the Judges was a dark era in Israel's history. It is interesting that the theme of the Judges is recorded twice in Judges 17:6 and 21:25. Both verses say, "In those days there was no king in Israel but every man did that which was right in his own eyes." Basically, the time period after Joshua was a period of lawlessness and rebellion. No man was personally trained to lead the country. Joshua missed a golden opportunity to invest in someone as Moses had invested in him.

SAMUEL AS A DISCIPLE-MAKER

After the period of Judges ended, we are introduced to another key man in the leadership of Israel: Samuel. Although Samuel had his weaknesses, it appears he played a key role in the oversight of the next leaders in Israel. His role was that of a prophet, but he seemed to do much more, including "disciple-making."

Samuel was the promised child to a woman who had been bereft of having a baby. First Samuel 1 describes her despair and God's subsequent promise to her. Samuel was given to the Lord for full-time service, and he was brought to the temple to be trained by Eli, the godliest man living at this time. Eli faithfully poured his life into Samuel, although he had no such success with his own sons. Eli's sons were evil and committed horrible sins. After God describes their behavior in 1 Samuel 2:12–17, He adds in verse 18, "But Samuel ministered before the LORD, being a child, girded with a linen ephod."

First Samuel 3:1 says, "And the child Samuel ministered unto the LORD before Eli." Chapter 3 explains how God called Samuel, and Eli had to lead him into the explanation of the call. Eli was able to take Samuel to this level of growth because God's hand was on Samuel. First Samuel 3 further adds in verse 19, "Samuel grew, and the LORD was with him." The next verse adds, "And Israel from Dan even to Beer-sheba knew that Samuel was established to be a prophet of the LORD." God's hand on Samuel, along with Eli's discipling, led Samuel to be one of the most influential leaders of his day. Eli dies in chapter 4, and not long after his death, Samuel takes the next phase of his leadership. He will influence the next two kings who will help establish the line of Christ as the True King. So, although Eli failed with his sons, the work of God continued through his work with Samuel.

It is not necessary to review all the examples of Samuel's leadership and oversight of the next two kings. They are clearly recorded in 1 and 2 Samuel. Samuel probably had more influence in the life of Saul than David, although Samuel also helped David. Before Samuel, the office of prophet was almost nonexistent. In Judges, only two are even given any recognition as those who stand in the gap for God (Judges 4:4 and 6:8). Samuel brought life into this call. Under Samuel's reign, at least two other prophets emerged who accepted key roles in the reign of David (Gad and Nathan). Maybe this explains Samuel's lesser role in David's reign. It is maybe somewhat assumptive to believe that Samuel influenced these men, but knowing Samuel, it seems to fit best with his mannerisms. In addition, Scripture clearly points out Samuel was appointed over the prophets, which suggests some form of leadership and mentoring program (1 Sam 19:20).

After Samuel's lead, we have numerous prophets who play key roles in all the life of Israel to the end of the Old Testament. The last seventeen books of the Old Testament are called the Major and Minor Prophets. There also are prophets who play key roles who do not have books named after them, including Elijah and Elisha.

ELIJAH AND ELISHA AS DISCIPLE-MAKERS

First Kings 19:19–21 records the call of Elisha by Elijah. Why did Elijah call him to follow? The text says that Elijah passed by Elisha and "cast his mantle upon him." Elijah was bidding Elisha to leave his earthly calling and become a prodigy under his leadership. Elijah was getting older, and the prophets needed someone to lead them after he was gone. Elijah went out and found his man. Verse 21 says that Elisha "arose, and went after Elijah, and ministered unto him." The call was a good call. He had his man, and the rest of the recorded story of Elisha proves that it was a good call.

Second Kings 2:1–3 explains some of the closeness the two enjoyed. Elijah realized that he was about to leave (verse 1), so he tells Elisha to remain behind while he goes on further. Elisha would have none of it. "As the Lord liveth, and as thy soul liveth, I will not leave thee. So they went down to Beth-el" (2 Kgs 2:2b). In the next verse, the sons of the prophets, who apparently knew about Elijah's departure, told Elisha about the fact that Elijah was about to leave. They said to Elisha that his master was about to be taken. Elijah had the role of master over Elisha. What was this role? Was it not personal mentoring to prepare him in what was to come? Elijah spent time investing into Elisha for the call of God to go forth. Elisha's response was clear: "Yea, I know it; hold ye your peace" (2 Kgs 2:5). He seemed to say, "Yes, I know he is about to leave, but I would rather not talk about that right now." It seems to parallel to the New Testament when Jesus was preparing to leave and told His disciples to "let not [their] hearts be troubled." This is one of the hardest parts of the mentoring and discipling ministry. You invest in others and then have to leave, either via death or moving on to another calling. This parting can be such sweet sorrow. Sweet, because you know you have done the discipling well. Sorrow, because you have bonded deeply with your apprentice. This is part of the cost.

DISCIPLE-MAKING THROUGHOUT THE OLD TESTAMENT

Once the Law had been ingrained in the lives of the people by the priests who were there to make the Law a daily part of everyone's life, it seemed the prophets took a more universal role over the entire nation. The king, prophet, and priest formed a perfect triangle to ensure the people were on the right track and the nation was a bright light, preparing for the coming of Messiah. We know they failed at times, but when Jesus did come, He came to a nation that was yearning for something. The Old Testament leaders completed their task. The Scriptures were preserved so many would have access. The Law had been interpreted for the layman's understanding. Although there were many perversions with traditions and man-made laws, the nation was still ready, and the time was ripe for Messiah and the birth of the church. We will examine this in the following chapters.

The passion for disciple-making started with Abraham and continued throughout the Old Testament. It was the passion of transmitting truth orally and discipling followers to proceed to the next level in their walk with God. The work was finished, and although there was a time of quiet between the Testaments, the silence was broken by John the Baptist, who had been taught through the Old Testament and was now ready to prepare the way for Messiah. Disciple-making truly is rooted in the Old Testament.

3

New Testament Mandate

My name is Keith Surland. I am an associate pastor of Mount Airy Bible Church. My life story was portrayed on the radio drama *Unshackled*. I have been saved since mid-August 1983. My background before I came to the Lord was one of drug and alcohol abuse. I lived an irresponsible life before I was saved. Since the time I came to Christ in 1983, I have earned a Bachelor of Arts degree from Arlington Bible College in 1989. I also married a pastor's daughter, Cheri Washburn, on August 5, 1989. I have been blessed not only with a tremendous wife, but also with two wonderful children named Ethan and Alethea.

I was a self-employed furniture refinisher from 1980 to 2004. In the fall of 2000, I enrolled in Capital Bible Seminary. My purpose was to earn a master's degree so I could teach somewhere. As God blessed my education, I escalated the amount of courses I took. With the help of my in-laws, I became a full-time student. I decided to graduate in the spring of 2004. I ran into a problem in January 2004. I needed to fulfill an internship in a church if I was to graduate that spring.

I would find a church and all looked promising, and then the church would, at the last minute, change its mind. Finally, a pastor agreed to let me work in his church. This church was small. I would not be allowed to preach or teach Sunday school. There would, in fact, be little I could do except visitation and working in the AWANA program. I did not care as long as I could fulfill my hours required for the internship. Late January in 2004, my professor, Dr. Ken Quick, told me he had a church where I could serve my internship. He said, "I found you a church to work in. It is Mount Airy Bible Church. Pastor Wally Webster is the senior pastor. They want someone who will teach Greek. They will compensate you financially, and this could possibly lead to a full-time position." I was delighted to hear this. It sounded too good.

I went to meet with Pastor Wally on the last Wednesday of February. He seemed reluctant to take me on as an intern, since he was quite busy at the time. He did not want to take on an intern if he could not give him quality time. Then all of the sudden he said, "Okay, let's do it." He took out a planner and charted out what I was to do for the next two months.

I really began to bond with the members of Mount Airy Bible Church. I was allowed to preach on several Wednesday prayer meeting nights. The most exciting thing to me was when I was asked to preach on a Sunday morning. I also taught some eager students the rudiments of New Testament Greek and a host of other projects.

Within two weeks of my internship, I noticed something different about the men in Mount Airy Bible Church. As Pastor Wally and I had our weekly meeting, I said, "The men in this place seem different. They are really involved in spiritual things. There are some really good men here." Pastor Wally told me, "I came to the conclusion that the church has misplaced its emphasis for so many years. I realized we need to invest in male leadership. So I began a program for men's discipleship."

When my internship came to a close, I felt sad. I did not want to leave my new church family at Mount Airy Bible Church. I had developed some ties with the people. Yet, I knew I had to get back to running my business. Work at the shop was piling up. I planned on going back to the shop full-time once I graduated from seminary. About a week and a half from graduation from Capital Bible Seminary, Pastor Wally took Cheri and me into his office. The elders were in the office waiting. In the presence of the elders, Pastor Wally handed me a generous love offering, thanked me for my internship, and asked me to come on board as an associate pastor.

I was speechless. For one thing, I did not think I was fit to be an associate pastor in any capacity. I was very flattered that I was even considered. Second, I did not want to close down the Refinishing Master business after twenty-four years of faithful operation. It was one of the most difficult decisions I ever made in my life. After some hard thinking and prayer, I decided to close my business and come on board the pastoral staff at Mount Airy Bible Church. The Lord did make my decision a little easier. You see, I suddenly became allergic to the many chemicals and solvents in my shop! Now there would be no turning back.

One thing Pastor Wally wanted me to do was to take a year of the Men with a Mission program. It is true that by this time I had about eight years of formal training in theology and biblical languages. Yet the Men with a Mission program helped me to see the practical side of men's issues as the men in the program seek to learn and understand the Bible and be all that God has for them.

Why is Men with a Mission a success? It's a success because it is biblical. Men need to be challenged to live above the mediocrity of this world. I have seen the quality of many of these men. I have seen them and their wives gleam with pride as they consummate three years of study in their graduation ceremony. They recognize that they followed and obeyed Christ's call to their studies.

When Jesus called His disciples, He called twelve ordinary men to do supernatural work.

The Men with a Mission program works because Jesus is still calling men to leave the fishing nets of this world and to follow Him. The emphasis of the Men with a Mission program is following Jesus. In so doing, the men often withhold gratification in their lives so they can follow Jesus with more focus. But the emphasis is never on what they give up but on the Lord whom they follow.

—Personal testimony of Keith Surland
Associate Pastor, Mount Airy Bible Church

IT DOES NOT TAKE long when reading through the New Testament to see our Lord had a clear agenda. He planned to teach the multitudes, minister to their many needs, go to a cross, die for the sins of the world, and put His entire plan in the hands of a chosen group of men. An old fable highlights this. It is said when Jesus returned after His time on earth, the angels asked how things went. He described His entire mission, and they asked Him what was next. He explained that He had left the entire mission in the hands of His disciples. The angels were most perplexed. Was He seriously putting His entire trust in these kinds of hands? Of course we know the Holy Spirit would dwell in each of them (Rom 8:9), but for the most part, it was left in the hands of the twelve. What a masterful plan it was; it was thorough, and because of those twelve men, we today hold these truths dear to our hearts.

THE CALL

Jesus was careful with His process. He, with His Father, had carefully designed this plan: He was to come to Earth and pay for the sins of mankind (1 Pet 1:19–20). This carefully constructed plan was a message of love from Him to a sinful world. "For God so loved the world, that He gave His only begotten Son, that whosoever believeth in him should not perish, but have everlasting life" (John 3:16). This verse is key for many. It demonstrates how much He loves us—such an extreme. Maybe for a righteous man some would die, but for sinners (Rom 5:7)? God, however, did so (Rom 5:8). All this was planned before the foundation of the world (Rev 13:8).

The New Testament describes the birth of our Lord. He was prophesied in the Old Testament and positively announced by a forerunner who prepared His way. Angels, shepherds, and wise men further promoted His coming, but to little avail to His people. He came unto His own and His own received Him not (John 1:12). After His birth, He remained in relative obscurity until thirty years of age. It was at this point in His life that Jesus was announced publicly by John the Baptist.

The gospel of John highlights this best when it records the words of John the Baptist, who proclaimed Jesus as "the Lamb of God, which taketh away the sin of the world" (John 1:29). This idea of Jesus as a lamb is well documented throughout the Old Testament. I believe it was a lamb that was slaughtered to cover Adam and Eve. I suggest this because Abel offered such a sacrifice, and there had been no teaching that a lamb was ever to die. Although a lamb is not specified, it is clear later in the Old Testament that a lamb was the offering of choice.

Abraham was prevented from sacrificing his son, Isaac (Gen 22), and a lamb was offered instead. Altars and sacrifice were the norm for many activities in the lives of the patriarchs. When Israel fled from Egypt, God taught them to kill a lamb and sprinkle the blood on the doorway of their homes as a sign of the covering of blood (Exod 12). Again, it is a lamb that comes into full view. The lamb is scattered throughout the sacrificial system, and it is a lamb that is symbolized in Isaiah 53 to describe our forthcoming relationship with Messiah. John picks up on the imagery and calls Jesus the "Lamb of God." This picture continues through Revelation, where it becomes the dominant picture used by John to describe our Lord. No wonder John the Baptist's perspective is critical.

Jesus is not only the Lamb; He also is the Shepherd. The Old Testament gently laid the foundation for this vision. Many of the great men of God were shepherds. One of the greatest Psalms describes our Lord as our Shepherd (Ps 23). There are many other allusions to shepherding, sheep, and the entire shepherding experience. In the New Testament, Jesus is also pointed out and described as a shepherd. He talks about Himself as the Good Shepherd in John 10. The writer of Hebrews calls Him the Great Shepherd (Heb 13:20), and Peter calls Him the Chief Shepherd (1 Pet 5:4). It is this position that He so beautifully carved out during His time here. Although He taught, healed, and ministered to many people, His shepherding of the twelve was major in communicating all He had done, said, and wanted continued. He carefully shepherded these men so they were able to fully communicate all He wanted. By modeling the example, He gave them the knowledge to accept what He wanted. The apostles were not just armed with information; they were also impacted by a life. I believe this concept of investing in the lives of leaders is greatly neglected, and it is causing such a drift in the church.

We point to many problems with the church today as if these are the reasons we are the way we are. Some say the church is too seeker-sensitive. Some say the church is too worldly. Some say the church is too liberal. Some say the church has lost its moorings. We can go and on. I agree the church has some problems; it always will as long as men are involved. The church is a body of fallen sinners saved by grace who often revert back to old habits and ideas (Rom 7). We are often too conformed to this world (Rom 12:1–2). We must stop focusing on what is wrong with the church and focus on what is right. You must do your part. Jesus said He will build His church, and the gates of hell will not prevail against it (Matt 16:18). This is good enough for me. We need to discover His ways, His plans, and His methods, follow them with His leadership, and watch Him bless His church. It is His model of shepherding that I believe we need to return to and make a major part of our church today.

Pastors today are too busy watching movie clips to use in their contemporary message, worried they might not be relevant. They are too preoccupied with the newest idea that might come out of some mega church and too focused on what is working in the secular world. Pastors today are too sensitive that using words such as sin, repentance, and conviction may make their message unpalatable. If we poured our God-given energy into the master example of Jesus and watched and modeled His life, we would be far more "successful" in reaching this world for Christ. The church is Jesus's plan, idea, ministry, passion, and love. He was fully God then and is fully God now. He has always been fully God. The church needs to minister as modeled by Jesus and stop letting the sinful world of man dictate the passion.

I have heard many of the statements and read many of the books about the need to adjust to our culture. I am not so narrow-minded that I am willing to die for methodologies. Methods are man-made. I understand the need for relevancy. Pastors need to be "contemporary" in thought so they are not so far outdated they cannot communicate with their audience. Remember, Jesus's methodologies will never be outdated and will never be obsolete (Matt 5:18). His word stands as sure today as when He first delivered it. There is nothing more pragmatic than doing church Jesus's way. This is a call to get back to the basics.

After Jesus's formal public introduction (His baptism) and His seminary training (forty days in the wilderness), He then began His ministry. What was His first plan of action? Choosing His followers (Matt 4:18). I realize many of us are not able to walk around and call on strangers to just leave their jobs and come and follow us. This would not be accepted in our society, nor is it really the point. The point Jesus makes is the importance of prayerfully choosing men to follow us. What do pastors do with their time today? Sermon preparation is usually one that takes up much of pastors' time, and rightfully so. The rest of our time is spent on what? Luncheons with the senior citizens? Counseling marriages that never seem to change? Board (bored) meetings? Hanging out with other pastors to hear about their griping and complaining about their sheep? What should we expect? They are sheep like us, right? What if we put our energy in the same work that Jesus did? Sounds radical, does it not?

Matthew 4 records right after Jesus was tempted; He continued preaching the Kingdom message. As He went from town to town, He sought chosen men. We see Him in Matthew 4:18 by the Sea of Galilee calling two brothers, Peter and Andrew. They were casting their nets because they were fishermen. Jesus called them to follow Him and He would make them "fishers" of men. Jesus knew He needed to surround Himself with those into whom He could invest His life. He knew His time here was going to be brief. None of us know the exact hour when we will be called home. We too need to keep our brevity of life in view. James says our life is a vapor (Jas 4:14). We will leave this earth one day, and only what is done for Christ will last. We need to live with this view in mind. With His view to train others, He first had to choose those who were to follow Him.

Mankind is always going to follow something. Gifted men in our churches today are leading Boy Scout troops, coaching sports teams, hunting endlessly, and golfing all over the world, and they claim they don't have time for disciple-making. We need to communicate that we are only here for a short time. Life is not about us. This is His world, and we need to fulfill the call of God on our lives. When we stand before God, our golf handicap is not going to be the grounds by which we are rewarded, nor the trophies on our mantels, but how we have used our lives (1 Cor 3:5–17). The men in our churches are going to fill their lives with things that keep them busy. We need to go after their time and challenge them about Kingdom business. Men are going to be busy, either way. Let's go after their energy for that which is truly satisfying and rewarding.

Jesus knew about mankind and went after them. Men need a higher call. My family and I have enjoyed attending plays, including *Les Miserables*. If you are not familiar with the story, let me pause for a short review. It is set during the time of the French Revolution when a small band of revolutionaries are trying to fend off the French Legion. They had little weaponry and very few men and they were fighting the established and well-equipped army of the French government. Their revolution was going to fail. One day one of the men returns to the barricade after visiting his love. He has that glazed look in his eyes from being distracted by his love. He is confronted immediately by the revolution leader and challenged with these words, "Marius, you're no longer a child. I do not doubt you mean well, but there is a higher call. Who cares about your lonely soul? We strive towards a larger goal. Our little lives don't count at all." [1]

As much as this play is a secular play, they have discovered the true meaning of Jesus's words when He called His followers to follow Him and reminded them of these things.

> Now when Jesus saw great multitudes about him, he gave commandment to depart unto the other side. And a certain scribe came, and said unto him, Master, I will follow thee whithersoever thou goest. And Jesus saith unto him, The foxes have holes, and the birds of the air have nests; but the Son of man hath not where to lay his head. And another of his disciples said unto him, Lord, suffer me first to go and bury my father. But Jesus said unto him, Follow me; and let the dead bury their dead (Matt 8:18–22).
>
> Then said Jesus unto his disciples, If any man will come after me, let him deny himself, and take up his cross, and follow me. For whosoever will save his life shall lose it: and whosoever will lose

---

1. Billig, *Les Miserables*.

his life for my sake shall find it. For what is a man profited, if he shall gain the whole world, and lose his own soul? Or what shall a man give in exchange for his soul? For the Son of man shall come in the glory of his Father with his angels; and then he shall reward every man according to his works. Verily I say unto you, There be some standing here, which shall not taste of death, till they see the Son of man coming in his Kingdom (Matt 16:24–28).

And there went great multitudes with him: and he turned, and said unto them, If any man come to me, and hate not his father, and mother, and wife, and children, and brethren, and sisters, yea, and his own life also, he cannot be my disciple. And whosoever doth not bear his cross, and come after me, cannot be my disciple. For which of you, intending to build a tower, sitteth not down first, and counteth the cost, whether he have sufficient to finish it? Lest haply, after he hath laid the foundation, and is not able to finish it, all that behold it begin to mock him, Saying, This man began to build, and was not able to finish. Or what king, going to make war against another king, sitteth not down first, and consulteth whether he be able with ten thousand to meet him that cometh against him with twenty thousand? Or else, while the other is yet a great way off, he sendeth an ambassage, and desireth conditions of peace. So likewise, whosoever he be of you that forsaketh not all that he hath, he cannot be my disciple. Salt is good: but if the salt have lost his savour, wherewith shall it be seasoned? It is neither fit for the land, nor yet for the dunghill; but men cast it out. He that hath ears to hear, let him hear (Luke 14:25–35).

Some men say, "That was then. Things are different today." I beg to differ. We are still bought with a price, and we are not our own (1 Cor 6:19–20). We are involved in a higher call. Our little lives do not count at all, unless they are embedded in the work of the Kingdom. Jim Elliott, the missionary who lost his life in Ecuador in 1956, said it well, "He is no fool who gives what he cannot keep, to gain what he cannot lose."[2] We need to call the men of the church to this higher calling. Our post-modern culture has changed in such a way that the call of sacrifice, consecration, and commitment is nearly lost. It does not appear in our newer books, songs, or messages. Jesus's call has not changed, nor will it ever. Do not think that any sacrifice for Him will go unrewarded.

Peter pondered this same question during a conversation with Jesus. Notice in Mark 10:28–31:

2. White, *Jim Elliott*, 63.

Then Peter began to say unto him, Lo, we have left all, and have
followed thee. And Jesus answered and said, Verily I say unto you,
There is no man that hath left house, or brethren, or sisters, or
father, or mother, or wife, or children, or lands, for my sake, and
the gospel's, But he shall receive an hundredfold now in this time,
houses, and brethren, and sisters, and mothers, and children, and
lands, with persecutions; and in the world to come eternal life. But
many that are first shall be last; and the last first (Mark 10:28–31).

Jesus never missed the opportunity. Sacrifice was His call. Today,
professing believers sometimes miss church because it is their son's third
birthday, or Auntie is having everyone over, or they don't want to miss
their children's games; the list continues ad nauseam. I am sure that we all
have heard it before. We are rearing a generation of children who see no
sacrifice modeled for Christ and who are never asked to do so themselves.
Do we believe this child-centered view is going to produce servants for
the King? It certainly will *not*.

Jesus called twelve men to Himself to sacrifice, serve, and eventually
die for the cause. He was not promoting a, "I have something good, easy,
fun, and you won't want to miss it" view. I see church offered this way all
the time. One church near us advertises that church is "coffee, doughnuts,
and a movie." And then they add, "I bet you never thought church would
be like this." No I didn't, and neither does Scripture. I can imagine Jesus
calling His disciples to follow Him for a bagel, some wine, and a chariot
race. Where is the call to surrender? Once again, I have heard that we are
reaching a post-modern culture that needs to be cautiously led into all
this. Maybe there is room for sensitivity in the process, but this approach
to reach others has filtered into the church and affected commitment as
well. Few churches require membership, ministry, or accountability. Are
we not letting our post-modern culture dictate our church?

We need to step up as men in the church and be counted as ones
who are going to accept this call on our lives. God has ordained it this
way, and we need to see it as our calling and responsibility. The church
has too long neglected men. We have excellent children's programs and
women's ministries. The church often baits these groups to eventually get
Dad into the flow. I believe the order is out of sorts. I see no wrong in
having excellent children and women's ministries; however, they are not
to be used as bait.

Men see through such a plan anyway. They are not ignorant. Men are willing for the church to lead their children (if it makes them better) and their wives (especially if it makes them submit), and they have no commitment. They can fish, hunt, golf, or whatever. It may be a door to these men, but I believe too often these other callings will so exhaust the church's time that the men will never be reached. Jesus picked up children and touched women, but He went after twelve men. Will you be a man to step up? Pastors need to make this a priority. Go after the men. Call them to commitment. If you do not get their time, someone else will, and it is doubtful it will be a spiritual quest should the world win. We need to realize that the laziness of the men in our ministries is also our responsibility. We are our brother's keeper. Just think of all the times Scripture calls us to reach out to one another.

> John 13:34—love one another
> Romans 12:5—members one of another
> Romans 12:10—in honor preferring one another
> Romans 14:19—one may edify another
> Romans 15:14—admonish one another
> Galatians 5:13—by love serve one another
> Galatians 6:2—bear ye one another's burdens
> Philippians 2:3—esteem others better than themselves
> James 5:16—pray one for another

There are twenty-five different positive "one anothers" in the New Testament that call us to go outside of ourselves and meet the needs of our fellow man. Because of all the problems that can occur between the sexes, I believe it is best for a man to go after a man in this regard—men reaching out to men, men encouraging men, men exhorting men. Promise Keepers is an enormous movement in our time. Why? The men are being neglected in the church. Men are being neglected in the community. Men need men. This is why Jesus called men to follow and then sent them out in pairs, not on bicycles and dark suits, but in connectedness. The call was clear from the lips of our Lord, and I believe it has sadly faded today in the halls of the church.

THE CLASSROOM

After Jesus called His twelve, He took them through three years of intense seminary training. Everything that Jesus did during the next three years had a direct impact on these twelve. He even took three of them, Peter, James, and John, on certain ventures designed especially for them alone: a healing situation, a mountaintop experience, and into the inner prayer time of Gethsemane. These three men are the pillars of the church (Gal 2:9), and they clearly understood their call. Overall, He was focused on training up twelve men to continue the work after His departure. The work was masterful. These twelve men—Judas was replaced by Matthias in Acts 1—turned the world upside down and today, we enjoy our Savior because of the incredible work they did. The work did not stop with them. They understood their call. They passed it on, and those they passed it on to passed it on, until it eventually became fruit in our lives. Will we pass it on? Will the next generation enjoy the fruit of this calling, or will a generation rise up who does not know Jesus?

Just think of how many times Jesus took His twelve into situations and taught them. He took them into all countries, nationalities, and peoples. He ministered to men, women, and children. He crossed boundaries, races, nationalities, and economic status. He ate with publicans and sinners, allowed sinners to be near Him, and modeled strength under control throughout. Many times His disciples must have left situations scratching their heads. This three-year intensive training session was going to change their lives forever. I often hear teachers say it was the resurrection that changed their lives from wimps to God-fearing men. I concur that the resurrection was monumental, but the resurrection was not in a vacuum. He invested three intensive years into these men that helped formulate all that they became after the resurrection. The resurrection simply jump-started their hearts, but the two coincide.

I recommend every church have some kind of "classroom" in place for the men to receive intensive training. I believe men want to be effective with their lives. I believe men want to be better fathers, husbands, workers, servers, and Christians, but they need guidance, and the church has to be the place. Many men receive their guidance in other places when the church ought to be the training ground. This is the path on which God led me several years ago as I was stumbling through the ministry. Our church was growing fast, and the needs of the people were greatly increasing. Families needed help with parenting; marriages needed assistance. The cries were coming often and regular, but we chose to go after a different group—the men. We still did what we could with the needs of the people, but we were careful not to exhaust our energy on that which was not lasting. The old saying still holds true, "Give a man a fish; you have fed him for today. Teach a man to fish, and you have fed him for a lifetime." We decided as a church to go after tomorrow with a vengeance. We believed the men needed to be trained first and foremost. It was Jesus's plan. It worked for Him, and I must add that it has greatly blessed us. I do not believe the children are the future of the church. I believe the men are the future of the church. Train them up and the rest will follow—so believed Jesus and the early church.

If you are a pastor, I plead with you to take this book and its resources to your board and beg them to come with you on this journey. Start with the existing board. Begin by investing in them during the next three years. Take them away for a retreat. Meet weekly or bi-weekly, and have a strategy. These are the men God has given to you, and they need it first and foremost. Even if they are seminary or similarly trained, do not let one of them escape this experience. You will need every person on board for this journey. By the way, if one leader is not with you, it will hurt you in the overall process. Move slowly and prayerfully.

If you are a layperson, put this book into your pastor's hands. Do not attempt to start something like this on your own without your pastor's direction. He is the shepherd of the flock. If this is going to be a help to the church, it must eventually come through him. Meet with him, and pray for him. Be willing to stay by his side and help. First and foremost, walk gently through this journey with him. God called the pastor to lead this ministry. You are simply the pastor's servant to help, not lead.

I will offer more suggestions for starting a training group. For now, I just want you to feel the passion. I am not sure there is a blessed "method" of how to accomplish this. The process is not as important as the calling. God may lead a church to do things far differently than I am suggesting, but we must not deviate from the call to train up faithful men. This is the mandate, and the method is open to discussion. I will suggest what God led us to do. If this in any way is a blessing to your church or ministry, then to God be the glory. It is just one beggar telling the other beggar where to find the bread. The glory all goes to the Bread Supplier.

Are you in a classroom training at this time? Most men are not. Most men are too busy with their world. Please keep in mind that if you name the name of Christ, you are not your own. You have no world. You have been bought with a price. Now glorify God with your body (1 Cor 6:19–20).

THE COMMISSIONING

Jesus did not expect His disciples to miss His point. He pressed it on their hearts in so many ways. He personally called the disciples. He prayed all night and then chose the twelve (Luke 6:12–13). He sent them out in pairs (Luke 10:1). He modeled before them, taught them, exhorted them, chastised them, and made them ready to face the foe. The greatest component of His commissioning of them came in His last times with them.

I believe it began in the "upper room" after James and John had been discussing who would sit on His right and left hand (Matt 20:20–28). Jesus challenged them that He did not come to be served, but to serve and give Himself as a ransom, and this came after all the disciples were debating who would take over after Jesus (Luke 22:24–27). It was following these episodes that we encounter John 13 and the washing of the disciples' feet. John 13 is an incredible example of the Master Teacher at work.

After the disciples argued about who was to be the greatest, Jesus took them into a specially prepared room, which the disciples themselves prepared. Luke records that it was Peter and John who actually prepared the room (Luke 22:8). They had been specifically sent by Jesus to take care of this; everything in the room would have been placed and organized by these two disciples. It is important that we reflect a little on the culture of the day. When guests would arrive, it was necessary to wash their feet as a matter of hospitality and cleanliness. The dinner guests ate while reclining, and their feet would easily be near the food and also near someone's nose. Without being too graphic, the roads and paths were not always clean from debris, if you know what I mean. Maybe this is where the Chinese get the "pu-pu platter"? Oh well, we must move on. It makes sense the basin and towel would have been at the door, but who was to do the washing?

Jesus was about to die. Someone needed to take over. Surely, if any disciple (Peter or John especially) took the lead and washed the feet, he would not have gotten the vote to be the leader. Servants were less than leaders, or at least this is what they thought. They were in for a classic lesson that would never leave them. Our Lord was about to teach them the importance of dying to self, which is the major hurdle for men in ministry. Somehow we believe that life is about us. What a shame, and what a loss to stand before the Lord in the final day and be ashamed, as 1 John 2:19 reminds us.

Jesus rose up from the table after everyone else had entered the room, stepped over to the basin and towel at which the disciples had thumbed their noses, and washed the disciples' feet. It is important to remember, in reference to the time of our Lord's ministry, when this act takes place. John is the only one who records this event and by chronology, it appears to be very near the end. It is one of the last things Jesus impressed on their minds. To say it as a preacher commonly says when closing his message, "If you forget everything else that I have said, please remember this point." Jesus obviously does not want them to forget anything He has taught them, but He especially wants them to retain His final acts.

After He washed their feet and had an interesting dialogue with Peter, He made some stirring comments in John 13:13–17.

> Ye call me Master and Lord: and ye say well; for so I am. If I then, your Lord and Master, have washed your feet; ye also ought to wash one another's feet. For I have given you an example, that ye should do as I have done to you. Verily, verily, I say unto you, the servant is not greater than his lord; neither he that is sent greater than he that sent him. If ye know these things, happy are ye if ye do them (John 13:13–17).

It is important to note this was the only time Jesus said He was leaving an example for them to follow. Why is this important? It highlights the overarching truths that Jesus had been teaching His disciples. It is the culmination of three years of modeling and teaching. The call is to die to self so you can be useful to the Master. Men are too committed to the pride of life (1 John 2:15–17) that decimates every call on their lives from the Master. This is why Jesus called them to die to their selves when they began to follow and called them to do the same as He was about to do. Jesus was about to entrust to these men the most important truths ever given to mankind. He was putting this sacred trust into their hands. They would pass the test only if they were already dead to their selfish ambitions.

Judas could not pass the test and chose a different path. The remaining eleven, with Matthias (Acts 1:26), accepted the call and invested their time by giving to others what had been given to them. This is the process of disciple-making. It can only happen when a person no longer views life through his eyes but through the call of God on his life. Men need to see this call and accept it as their path. Churches need to promote it and pastors need to die keeping it in focus. What does it profit a man if he gains the whole world and loses his soul (Matt 16:26)? And what does it profit to give one's entire life to that which is only wood, hay, or straw, to see it go up in smoke as worthless (1 Cor 3:12–13)? Count the cost and run the eternal race well.

After this remarkable time of self-sacrifice teaching, Jesus laid down His life for His sheep. The cross was ahead for Him, and He needed to finish the race. He came to lay down His life. No one took it from Him. The question lately has been, "Who killed Jesus?" This is a foolish question, because no one killed Jesus. He gave up His life, and if we label anyone for His death, we would have to label our sins as the cost, and it was the Father who actually took His life (Isa 53:4). After His death, Jesus spent three days in the tomb and was afterward raised from the dead. He actually died and came back to life. This is the teaching of the New Testament and the belief that Paul taught. He is alive so we can also live (1 Cor 1:5).

Jesus commissioned His disciples during an important time of teaching just before His ascension. Matthew 28:18–20 often is called the Great Commission. It truly is an amazing commissioning of the disciples by the Risen Lord. Notice the wording of this incredible passage:

> And Jesus came and spake unto them, saying, All power is given unto me in heaven and in earth. Go ye therefore, and teach all nations, baptizing them in the name of the Father, and of the Son, and of the Holy Ghost: Teaching them to observe all things whatsoever I have commanded you: and, lo, I am with you always, even unto the end of the world. Amen (Matt 28:18–20).

It seems in our time of missions and commissions, we have focused on verse 19 and the last of verse 20. We understand the going, the teaching, the baptizing, and that He is with us to the end, but we have missed the importance of the "teach" in verse 19 and of what He said in the beginning of verse 20. The word used here for "teach" is better translated as "make disciples." This is not the same as "make converts." He is not suggesting that our mission is evangelism, although this is inherent. We are truly to reach the lost with the gospel of Jesus.

We have been given the ministry of reconciliation, no doubt, but there is something more inherent in this disciple-making process than is first evident. The word used for "make disciples" is the major word used in the New Testament for disciple. It is found only in Matthew, Mark,

Luke, John, and Acts, and it is what Jesus devoted His entire life to. It is taking a follower and making him or her like Himself. A disciple was never looked at as simply a follower. A disciple was considered to be one who gave up his life to follow. It was the mark of the follower that he was a disciple. Disciples were not called Christians until Acts 11:26. To be a disciple of Jesus was not to be just a follower, a joiner, or one who has just signed up. Jesus said if you want to be my disciple, you must see life not as your own. Luke confirms this in Luke 14:26–33.

> If any man come to me, and hate not his father, and mother, and wife, and children, and brethren, and sisters, yea, and his own life also, he cannot be my disciple. And whosoever doth not bear his cross, and come after me, cannot be my disciple. For which of you, intending to build a tower, sitteth not down first, and counteth the cost, whether he have sufficient to finish it? Lest haply, after he hath laid the foundation, and is not able to finish it, all that behold it begin to mock him, Saying, This man began to build, and was not able to finish. Or what king, going to make war against another king, sitteth not down first, and consulteth whether he be able with ten thousand to meet him that cometh against him with twenty thousand? Or else, while the other is yet a great way off, he sendeth an ambassage, and desireth conditions of peace. So likewise, whosoever he be of you that forsaketh not all that he hath, he cannot be my disciple (Luke 14:26–33).

If there was any doubt about what Jesus understood a disciple to be, Luke 14:26–33 should clear it up.

A closer look at Matthew 28:20 reveals a section of this commission that is often overlooked. Notice that Jesus said His twelve were to be "teaching them [the disciples who were going to follow from verse 19] to observe all things whatsoever I have commanded you." Jesus was specifically stating they were to teach the followers, disciples, converts, or whatever word you choose, the material and lifestyle they had just received from Him personally. Jesus was only here for three years. He had no plans to return, call twelve more men, personally teach them, and then go back. This would be nonsense.

Instead, He invested in the twelve so they could do what He had done, only in a greater measure. This was exactly what He promised when He said, "Greater works than these shall he do, because I go to my Father" (John 14:12). The "he" in this verse refers to the followers after Jesus. The twelve were to go forth and call men to follow Jesus the same as though He were here and doing it Himself—which He was through them. The twelve were to take them through the classroom of training—just like they had personally experienced—and send them out to go forth and do the same. It is His perfect plan that many through the years have accepted and modeled. Your faith stands as a testament to this grand truth. We will see later that the early church caught this vision and carried it out completely. Of course, church history could validate the church fathers' understanding, but for this study, we will keep to the inspired text.

The disciples were not told to teach the Law. The disciples were not told to teach the priesthood. The disciples were not told to teach the feasts, the Passover, or the traditions. They were told to teach what Jesus had taught them. They were told to take the converts through Christ's three-year seminary program. They were to teach them about forgiveness, love, holiness, passion, faith, etc. They were to teach them to observe (keep, obey, commit) these truths. Jesus did not spend three years with His men just to take up their time. It was an investment that was to be kept intact after He left. I believe all Scripture is given by the inspiration of God and is profitable for doctrine, reproof, correction, and the instruction in righteousness that the man of God may be mature, perfectly equipped to serve the Lord (2 Tim 3:16–17). But Jesus's disciples, the foundation of the church, were to teach the truths that He personally taught (Matt 28). This was their commission, and they took it seriously. Will we take this call as seriously, and will all who come after find us faithful?

4

Jesus to Peter

What a privilege it has been to be a part of the Men with a Mission class. Besides the 203 Bible verses that we were required to memorize and the fifty-one-plus topics that we covered throughout the three years, the Men with a Mission class has had the most significant impact on my Christian walk. The studies throughout the three years pushed and stretched me in directions that I never imagined possible.

Your teachings and personal life examples have given me what I call the bifocals of the faith. Not only do I now possess the abilities to discern and properly unearth and know the biblical truths, but I also know how I ought to live my life by the example that you have personally displayed.

Your dedication to teaching with your own life as a testimony has not only changed my life and the lives of the other students, but also, through a ripple effect, has enlightened the lives of my family, my friends, and everyone around me.

You have truly taught me how to live out 2 Timothy 2:2 and 2 Timothy 2:15. The Men with a Mission class has been a life-changing experience for me and to all those around me. I am forever grateful for your dedication and devotion. May God continue to bless your ministry.

—Personal testimony of Arn J. Halpin
Direct Electric Services, President
Chairman of Chair Ministry, Mount Airy Bible Church

Our church is growing, not only in size and membership, but also in knowledge imparted to men through the Men with a Mission training. Personally, I feel that what I have learned in how to handle Scripture and apply it to life has been a true blessing in my daily walk. This training has helped me be a better husband, father, and follower of Jesus Christ.

—*Personal testimony of Chris Brown*
Bettar Appliance Services, Appliance Technician
Deacon, Mount Airy Bible Church

THERE MAY NOT BE a more beautiful picture of our Lord's discipleship ministry than is found in His relationship with Peter. Although some have taken Peter's purpose far beyond the actual text, there is still a lot of material that supports that Jesus and he had an intimate relationship. Peter was clearly Jesus's most important disciple. Although John is called the disciple whom Jesus loved (John 21:7), and Jesus left His mother in the care of John, the evidence is overwhelming in the New Testament supporting Peter as the main disciple. The early church also seems to support this theory, as Peter takes on clear oversight in the first days after the ascension. As you will discover in Acts 1–6, Jesus discipled many, including the twelve and the three, but Peter was His man.

JESUS'S NUMBER-ONE DISCIPLE

Why do I think Peter is Jesus's number-one disciple and number-one project?

1. Scripture records that Jesus was only ever in Peter's house, not another disciple (Matt 8:14).

2. Peter is always listed first in all the lists found in the Gospel accounts (Matt 10:2 and Luke 6:14). Matthew 10:2 even says he is first.

3. Peter is clearly taken places that only two other disciples, James and John, are taken: the Mount of Transfiguration (Matt 17:1), the healing of Jairus's daughter (Mark 5:37), and the Garden of Gethsemane (Matt 26:37).

4. The New Testament mentions that Jesus personally called Peter from fishing (Matt 4:18). Not all of the disciples have this recorded about them.

5. Peter is the only disciple who walked on water (Matt 14:22–37). I realize one could argue that he was the only one who asked, but nevertheless, it still stands Peter was the only one. It also is interesting to note just how many times Scripture records that

Peter got out of the boat. He got out of the boat to follow initially (Matt 4:18) and to walk on water (Matt 14:22–33). He knelt in the boat to worship the Lord (Luke 5:1–11). After the resurrection, Peter went back to fishing, and when the Lord called from the shore and they got more fish, he jumped out again (John 21:7). No other disciple is ever recorded as getting out of the boat.

6.   He is the only disciple who asked for an explanation of the parables (Matt 15:15).

7.   He is the only one who is credited for the great confession about Christ (Matt 16:16). It is interesting that Jesus only asked Peter.

8.   He is the only disciple who the New Testament records as rebuking our Lord (Matt 16:22–23).

9.   When there was a "failure" to pay taxes by the disciples, those who received tribute money came to Peter (Matt 17:24). Consequently, our Lord sent Peter, the fisherman, out to catch a fish with a coin in its mouth to pay the taxes.

10.   Only Peter came to Jesus to ask about forgiveness (Matt 18:21).

11.   Only Peter came to Jesus to mention they had forsaken all to follow Him (Matt 19:27).

12.   Although all the disciples stated they would not betray Jesus, it is Peter who is recorded as the most vehement (Matt 26:33).

13.   Although all the disciples fell asleep, it is Peter who our Lord addressed (Matt 26:40). It is as if Peter was the captain of the inner circle.

14.   John was able to get into the inner court during the trial, but Peter was the only other disciple who was even near the events of Jesus's last hours (Matt 26:58). He followed from far off, but at least he followed.

15.   According to Scripture, Peter is the only disciple with a family member that Jesus healed (Mark 1:30).

16.   Peter was one of only three disciples who were surnamed. He was Simon who was surnamed Peter (Mark 3:16). Only James and John received surnames (Mark 3:17).

17.   Only Peter talked with Jesus about the fig tree (Mark 11:21).

18. Peter joined with three other disciples, James, John, and Andrew, to discuss the end times with Christ (Mark 13:3).

19. Peter's boat is the only boat Scripture ever identifies that Jesus was actually in (Luke 5:1–11).

20. Luke mentioned Peter as the one who spoke up when Jesus asked, "Who touched me" (Luke 8:45)?

21. Peter and John are the only two who got the privilege to prepare the Passover (Luke 22:8).

22. According to Scripture, Peter was the only disciple during the trials that Jesus looked at (Luke 22:61).

23. Only two disciples ran to the tomb—Peter and John—although John, who was younger, outran Peter (Luke 24:12).

24. Peter was one of few disciples that we know of his hometown (John 1:44).

25. Only Peter asked Jesus, "To whom shall we go? thou hast the words of eternal life" (John 6:68).

26. Although Jesus washed all the disciples' feet, only Peter is recorded in a dialogue with Jesus about foot washing (John 13:6).

27. Only Peter, during the supper, privately asked John to ask Jesus who was the betrayer (John 13:24).

28. Only Peter asked the Lord, "Why cannot I follow thee now?" (John 13:37).

29. Only Peter used a sword to protect Jesus in the garden (John 18:10), although at least one other disciple had a sword (Luke 22:38).

30. Peter led at least six other disciples back into fishing after the death of Jesus (John 21:3).

31. Only Peter had the three-fold test by Jesus of questioning whether he really loved Jesus (John 21:15–17).

32. Only Peter was specifically told to feed Jesus's sheep (John 21:15–17).

33. Peter is the only disciple Jesus specifically told how He would die (John 21:18).

34. Only Peter asked how John was going to die (John 21:22).

35. Peter is one of the few disciples privileged to write a book in Scripture, along with John and Matthew.

36. Peter is the only apostle that Jesus specifically said He was praying for (Luke 22:31–32).

With all of this information about Peter, one can readily see that Jesus invested much personal time in him. Only John is given a few privileges to the level of Peter, with the oversight of Mary probably being the greatest. Nevertheless, it is Peter who stands above all others in sheer reference alone.

PETER'S DENIAL

There is one more area that we have to address about Peter. Peter's denial of the Lord is major. Jesus told him that he was going to deny the Lord three times, which he precisely did. Luke records that our Lord gazed on him at this time and that Peter went out and wept bitterly. Peter is truly a crushed and repentant man, but the story does not end here.

Mark 16:7 records two of the most encouraging words to Peter in all of Scripture. After Jesus rose from the dead, the women came to the tomb to anoint His body, not knowing He was not there. An angel appeared to them and told them, "He is risen; he is not here; behold the place where they laid him. But go your way, tell his disciples and Peter that he goeth before you into Galilee" (Mark 16:6–7). Those two words "and Peter" must have been extremely encouraging. He was the only disciple the angel mentioned and the only disciple who was singled out in the resurrection drama.

What was our Lord's point in singling out Peter? It had to be one of forgiveness and encouragement. Peter had already repented. It was time to go on, and Jesus had a plan for Peter. He was taking disciple-making with Peter to a new level. It was the path of second chances. We will face many disciples who have fallen short and have failed. We need to take them to Peter's example and move on. AWOL is not a good thing, and it is not the end. A righteous man falls down seven times, but gets up (Prov 24:16). You might feel a little like Peter yourself. It is time to repent and go forward, don't you think?

First Corinthians 15:5 mentions one more episode about the resurrection appearances. Paul says there was a post-resurrection appearance that Jesus made to Peter alone; yet, none of the Gospel accounts record such an event. I wonder if it was so moving it was an appearance only recorded in the heart of Peter. One thing is for certain—he never looked back. I can only imagine Jesus coming to Peter while he is weeping profusely, and Jesus kneels by him with a handkerchief and dries his tears. It must have been an amazing scene. I can see Him say, "Peter, I forgive you. Now, there is work of disciple-making to do."

PETER'S RE-COMMISSIONING

One final passage demands our attention before we finish with Peter. John 21 records the three-fold interchange between Jesus and Peter. Jesus begins in John 21:15 with a question to Peter if he loved (agapaō) Him. Jesus uses the highest word for love in the Greek language. Peter responds with a lesser love word (phileō). Jesus asks him a second time with the same word, and Peter responds with the same weaker word back. Jesus asks a third time, using Peter's weaker word for love, and it grieved Peter. Obviously Jesus wanted Peter to really decide how serious he was about full devotion to Him. What Jesus wanted from Peter was going to be complete surrender and sacrifice—a confirmation of whether Peter was really committed. It is interesting that He asks Peter three times, comparable to Peter's three denials.

There is more in this passage. Jesus asks Peter in response to do something. Jesus tells Peter to feed and shepherd the lambs/sheep. In other words, Jesus is telling Peter that He wants Peter to be a shepherd and bring the sheep along. What is the responsibility of the shepherd but to make disciples? We will later see Scripture that supports this exact role of a disciple-maker—to tend the sheep. Peter was to set an example, and in Acts we see him take this role to the level God expected. Peter was to shepherd the flock, like Jesus did, and Peter would set the example for all disciple-making from his day forward.

Jesus discipled the twelve, specifically the three, but more intently the one, named Peter. Peter was His man. Peter was the investment, and it paid off greatly. He led the early church well and provided the necessary balance for Paul. They made the direction of the church to Jew and Gentile clear and precise. The church was going forward. Jesus paid the price and discipled the men, especially Peter. We are the beneficiaries of such work.

PETER AS A DISCIPLE-MAKER

Peter took this same approach to ministry. Although we have much more in the New Testament about Paul's disciple-making, Peter was a disciple-maker as well.

1. Acts 1:12—The disciples return to Jerusalem just as Jesus said
2. Acts 1:13—Peter is listed first
3. Acts 1:15—Peter takes over
4. Acts 2:14—Peter preaches the first message
5. Acts 2:37—Peter leads
6. Acts 2:38—Peter answers
7. Acts 3:1—Peter and John (notice who is listed first)

Acts also has many more examples of Peter's leadership. It appears he personally invested in Silas (1 Pet 5:12) and Mark (1 Pet 5:13). Many believe it was Peter who influenced Mark's writings and gave him much of the information to write the gospel of Mark. Peter caught the method of Jesus and applied it greatly to his years of ministry for the Lord. Peter gives way to Paul as the foremost disciple-maker, but history will reveal that Peter truly was our Lord's man, and he did it well. Was it not to Peter that Jesus gave the keys to the Kingdom? We owe much to the great work that Peter did for the early church.

5

Matthew 28:18–20

I was saved at the ripe old age of forty. Until that time, I had barely finished high school, had read one book cover to cover in my life, and had some serious comprehension issues. My desire as a new believer was to join a Bible study under the tutelage of Pastor Wally Webster. Pastor Wally, however, recommended the Men with a Mission discipleship class.

I was, of course, looking for a study where the pastor did all the work and I listened and learned. To my shock and surprise, I was actually required to study the Bible, read books, memorize Scripture, interact with others, and be held accountable. This three-year program was a comprehensive discipleship program including elements of theology, Bible study, ethics, and Christian practice.

Through this mentoring and discipleship program, I caught fire for the word of God and have grown substantially in the "grace and knowledge of my Lord and Savior Jesus Christ." After finishing the Men with a Mission program in 1998, I went on to earn a Bachelor's degree in theology in 2005 and am currently working on a Master's degree in biblical studies. I do not believe this would have been possible without the guardianship of Pastor Wally and his commitment to the Lord's commands to disciple others.

—Personal testimony of Ken Varney
Strober Building Supply, Corporate Sales

Pastor Wally's Men with a Mission discipleship program is truly life-changing. The evidence of this is the Men with a Mission graduates themselves—they are the fruit of Pastor Wally's labor. The Lord has most definitely rewarded Pastor Wally's obedience to the call of 2 Timothy 2:2.

Pastor Wally's teachings and counseling have had a huge impact on my life. A little over five years ago, MABC placed me under church discipline, for good reason. Today I am a full-time employee of our church and the school that is run by our church. This is a long story, but I give the credit to the three years I spent in the Men with a Mission program and the support I received from Pastor Wally and many other men of our church.

—Personal testimony of Robert Kelley
Mount Airy Bible Church and Christian Academy
Technology Manager

THE MOST IMPORTANT PASSAGE in all of Scripture on the subject of disciple-making is the last command of our Lord in Matthew 28:18–20. It has been called the Great Commission and is known by many who love the words of our Lord. Although it is known by most believers, it is clearly one of the least-obeyed commands of our Lord.

THE WORDS OF JESUS

When it comes to the words of our Lord, all believers are moved to a certain level of awe and respect. We revere everything He said, did, and especially the ground He walked upon. Every year millions of Christians travel to the Holy Land to see some of the great places where our Lord traveled and lived. It is supposed to be one of the most moving experiences one could ever have. I hope one day to be able to travel there and follow those sacred steps.

Because most followers cannot do this, we cherish Jesus's words. We have even developed a "red-lettered Bible," which highlights the words of Christ in red with all the other words in black. One might not say these words are more important than any other words, but there is a certain reverence to the red letters.

Jesus is often quoted in our everyday lives. Someone will say, "Didn't Jesus say . . ." Then they follow with a quote such as, "Judge not," "Love one another," or "It is more blessed to give than to receive." Sometimes Jesus is even quoted as if He said something that He did not. One such example is, "Do unto others as you would have them do unto you." Another misquote is, "Cleanliness is next to godliness." Nevertheless, Jesus is undoubtedly the most quoted religious leader of all times. Millions of books, songs, and articles are published yearly with the fingerprints of Jesus all over them. Several years ago there was a commercial about a man named E. F. Hutton. He was a financial guru, and when he spoke, people listened. It was filmed in places such as restaurants and when someone mentioned this man's name, everyone stopped what they were doing to listen. Jesus is quoted and respected far more, and even to this day when someone says, "But didn't Jesus say . . ." it still captures attention.

Unfortunately, we have selectively chosen which words of Jesus we want to quote and which words we want to ignore. I believe His last command may be the most misunderstood and most ignored of all of His words. When it comes to the actual obedience of this last command, one would wonder if the church might have just lost the last chapter of Matthew altogether.

Maybe it is simply misunderstood. Perhaps many believers today have concluded these words were really only for the twelve. Maybe they were intended for the early church alone and really have no effect on us today. I beg to differ. I believe His last command on earth is a command for us today, as well as all of Jesus's commands. Possibly a closer look at this command will reveal this.

Acts 1:4 is a command for the disciples to wait for the promise of the Father, who would enable them to carry out the command of Matthew 28. This was really part of the last command to go into all the world, and it is re-emphasized in Acts 1:8, "But ye shall receive power, after that the Holy Ghost is come upon you; and ye shall be witnesses unto me both in Jerusalem, and in all Judea, and in Samaria, and unto the uttermost part of the earth." Acts 1 was connected with Jesus's last words in Matthew 28—go into all the world and make disciples.

LOOKING CLOSER AT MATTHEW 28:18–20

Let's look closer at Matthew 28:18–20, "And Jesus came and spake unto them saying, All power is given unto me in heaven and in earth. Go ye therefore, and teach all nations [make disciples], baptizing them in the name of the Father, and of the Son, and of the Holy Ghost, Teaching them to observe all things whatsoever I have commanded you; and lo, I am with you always, even unto the end of the world. Amen."

First, it is important to note that this is a command. The main verb is in verse 19, which the KJV translates as "teach all nations," whereas the NASB and NIV use "make disciples." It is an imperative verb, and it is the main verb of the entire passage. The other verbs translated into English, go, baptize in verse 19, and teach in verse 20, are all participles, and they get the force of an imperative from the main verb, which is an imperative. It would seem that in English, there are actually four imperatives: go, teach, baptize, and teaching. In a sense, this is true, but there is one main imperative verb that is found in verse 19—make disciples. To show how important this command was, the Holy Spirit inspired all four Gospel writers to include this command in their text. Although they are all somewhat different, the main idea of making disciples occurs in all four accounts (Matt 28:18–20, Mark 16:15–18, Luke 24:45–48, John 20:21). In addition, it is the only command of Jesus transferred to the early church in Acts.

I know you are running to look in Matthew through John to see what other commands are repeated in all four accounts. Let me save you the labor. There is only one other command that is repeated in all four accounts. It is the command that Jesus began His ministry with, "Follow me." It is found in Matthew 4:19, Mark 2:14, Luke 5:27, and John 1:43. Jesus's first and last commands are the only commands the Holy Spirit inspired to be in all four accounts. These two commands formulate the two critical components of disciple-making. First, is the commitment to follow. Second, is the commitment to be a part of the disciple-making process, which includes being discipled and committing to discipling others. This is disciple-making, and the curriculum needed is found within the two commands. Let's go back to Matthew 28.

The Greek word for "make disciples," which is actually one Greek word, although it is two English words, is *mathēteuō* and *manthanō*. This particular Greek word is only found four times in the New Testament (Matt 13:52, 27:57, 28:19, Acts 14:21). It basically means to make disciples. It is related to the Greek noun *mathētēs* which is the primary word in the New Testament for disciple, which is found 268 times. It is the word for Jesus's disciples. When you put a verb to this noun, you are actually saying it is the process of taking an ordinary man and making him a disciple like the work Jesus did on His men. It is the process that is the focus. To take this noun to a verb form is to say the noun is the goal. We are in the work of "discipling," making disciples, or discipleship. The goal is what Jesus did during His time.

THE PROCESS OF MATTHEW 28:18-20

What is unique about this command is that Jesus gives the exact process needed. He reveals the format of disciple-making in this passage. First, there is the "going" process. The participle suggests a translation of "as you are going." In other words, it is unthinkable that a disciple-maker is not going to the lost and telling them about Jesus. It is so sad to hear there are believers today who have never led anyone to Jesus. This thought is of the utmost concern. We are to be a going people. Israel of the Old Testament were God's people who were not to be going. They were to stay pure and unattached from all other peoples. The church is to be in the world, just not of the world. We have been sent. John 17:18 says it well when Jesus said, "As thou hast sent me into the world, even so have I also sent them into the world." This was new to the followers. They were to be a going people—going into the world.

Second, they were to be baptizing. We are to make disciples by going and baptizing. Why does Jesus include baptism in this process? What role does it have to play? Some have truly taken baptism far beyond its intent. Baptism does not save anyone, by birth or by adult baptism. Scripture is very clear. We are saved by grace through faith, not of ourselves; it is the gift of God, not of works, like baptism, lest we should boast (Eph 2:8–9).

Then why is baptism a part of the process? Because baptism is the outward sign that there has been an inward work. If you look all through the book of Acts, you will see just how baptism fits into the scheme of disciple-making. Notice the order in Acts 2:41a, "Then they that gladly received his word were baptized." They received the word (inward), and were baptized (outward). Acts 8 is another clear example. Philip went and preached to this Ethiopian and opened the Scriptures to him. He also must have discussed baptism with this man, because in Acts 8:36 as they were moving by water, the Ethiopian asked to be baptized. Philip was clear with him in the next verse, "If thou believest with all thine heart, thou mayest." In other words, if you have received it inwardly, you can do the outward rite of baptism. Baptism was the public display of the inward work.

Just as baptism has been taken too far to make it synonymous with salvation, there are those who have taken it far too lightly. Remember, Jesus included baptism in His last command and connected it with the mission of the apostles. We dare not take it lightly. Perhaps we should be more cautious as to how early we entertain candidates for baptism and exhort those who have never been baptized to be baptized. It is connected with Jesus's plan. Baptism says that a new believer is completely immersed in Jesus and ready to do His bidding. This action leads us into the third part of disciple-making.

The third component to this process is found in Matthew 28:20. A disciple-maker is one who teaches (different word than in verse 19) the baptized follower to observe (keep/obey) all things that Jesus commanded. Jesus did not give the material to the disciples in a written form. They experienced it. Jesus personally gave them the curriculum through their three years with Him, and we cannot stress enough how important these three years with Christ were. Remember when they replaced Judas? They chose two men who had been with Jesus during those critical three years (Acts 1:21–22). Also, remember that Paul went through a similar teaching experience, as explained in Galatians 1. The disciple-making process was a process that required the disciple to spend intentional time with Jesus for the length of three years. The early church was to disciple-make the same way. Let disciples be with you, and teach them about Jesus. This is what we saw in the early church. Now that the foundational apostles have died off and we have the completed Scriptures, we too are to disciple-make and use the entire word.

A disciple, then, is one who has been taught about Jesus, and in particular, one who has been taught to obey Him. We are to teach them to obey all things that Jesus has commanded. Jesus is looking for a life of obedience. This is why, when we come to Him, it begins with dying to self—no longer my life, but thine. He promises in Matthew 28:20 that He will be with us, even to the end. There are only two times where Jesus specifically promises His presence. First, He promises His presence in the church discipline process found in Matthew 18:15–20. Second, He promises His presence in the disciple-making process, "And lo, I am with you always, even unto the end of the world" (Matt 28:20). These are two neglected components of the church today.

JESUS MODELED MATTHEW 28:18–20

Not only does Jesus promise His presence, but He has also provided His example to observe and learn. The exciting thing about His process is that it works! Why should any pastor want to "do church" differently than the Master Builder? Disciple-making was His passion, and He passed the importance of this mission on to His followers to go and do the same. This is what the Great Commission is all about.

Notice how He did this. First, He modeled the importance of "going." No follower of His will ever be asked to go anywhere or do anything that will come close to the level of commitment that Jesus made for us in coming to this earth. He left the glory of heaven, took upon Himself the form of a servant, and died the death of a common criminal (Phil 2:6–8). He will never ask us to go to the extreme He did, but He is asking us to go. We are to go to our neighbors, co-workers, classmates, friends, family, and whoever else He brings into our path, even into the entire world. It is the first part of the process. We need to be ready to go at any time. We are on twenty-four/seven stand-by. We await His beckoning call.

Second, He brought people to a place of commitment. Jesus personally did not baptize anyone (John 4:2), but His disciples did. He personally asked people to follow Him. All through His teaching He called people to get out of the boat, leave the dead, leave their riches, leave their families, and follow Him. We too must bring people to a place of commitment. Will you give your life to Christ today?

Third and last, He personally discipled men. It is recorded in Scripture where He worked with the twelve, worked with the three, and of course, worked with Peter. His whole life was fully devoted to these men. He finished it well, and then they took what He commanded them and taught faithful men to go and do likewise. These faithful men have done the same and now here we are, two thousand-plus years later. The question remains—will those who have gone before have labored in vain in their investment in us?

EXEGESIS OF MATTHEW 28

Just how important is this command? First, it is one of only two commands that are repeated in all four of the gospel accounts. Only the command to "follow me" is also repeated as such. Second, it is the last command Jesus gave to His disciples. In this command, He included all the rest that He had spoken. This last command brings all the other commands together. Third, it is the only command where He gives us the exact details of how to get it accomplished. He offers many commands, but in this one He gives explicit details: go, baptize, and teach. Fourth, it is the only command where He gives us all the tools necessary to accomplish the task. He gave the commands and the Holy Spirit, who was to ensure all the commands were remembered and gave the power necessary to teach them and obey them. Fifth, He modeled this command in detail while He was here. He came (representing the sending of the disciples), He brought people to a place of commitment (which is to happen at baptism), and He taught them His commands (exactly what He has asked us to do).

No other command of our Lord has this level of importance. How can we overlook the serious call to be a disciple-maker any longer? We need to realize people are going to live forever somewhere, and those who have faith in Christ are going to give an account of their lives. We want to present them, as Paul said to the Corinthians, as "chaste virgins." We need to accept our call to be our brother's keeper.

6

The Early Church Caught It

When I first entered Men with a Mission, I was deficient in many basic Bible skills, which led me to question early on whether I could keep up with the course or continue at all. Ultimately, I decided to continue. This was probably the first of many good decisions I've made as a result of taking this program!

I can categorize the benefits of this program in two ways. First are the basic intellectual tools for comprehending and communicating Scripture. Such lessons helped me immensely.

The second category, which provided even greater value, encompasses the deeper lessons that impact my conduct as a Christian, husband, father, employee, etc. It is difficult to condense three years worth of these lessons into a few words. However, if I had to select just one, it would undoubtedly be the principle of "dying to self."

Acceptance of God's will over my own underlies so many of the principles examined in this program. It has also affected many important decisions in my life. This simple, but often difficult to implement, step lies on the critical path to achieving so much of what God wants for me.

I owe many thanks to many people. Thanks to Pastor Wally for his vision for and commitment to this program; to those who supported him in crafting and teaching classes; to my prayer partners who helped me stay focused; and especially to my wife, Jennifer, who helped me make room for all this in an already hectic schedule. This is yet another example of what happens when many people work together in the Christian body, inspired by God.

—Personal testimony of John Farrell
Omen, Inc., Information Assurance Research Analyst

AFTER THE ASCENSION, THE disciples did not fall into frenzy and worry about what was next for them to do. They set out to obey the

Lord's direction for them and to not let His investment into their lives be for naught. Their first directive was to go to Jerusalem and wait for the promise of the Father (Acts 1:8). This was the coming of the Holy Spirit. The Holy Spirit was not indwelling every follower up to this point. He had been assigned certain tasks throughout time, but there was no permanent or collective indwelling of the followers. This would all change in Acts 2 at Pentecost, where the Holy Spirit came down upon the followers of Christ. After this point, the Holy Spirit would be a permanent companion of those who chose to follow.

ACTS 2: PENTECOST AND DISCIPLE-MAKING

Acts 2:41–47 begins to describe the action of the early church:

> Then they that gladly received his word were baptized: and the same day there were added unto them about three thousand souls. And they continued stedfastly in the apostles' doctrine and fellowship, and in breaking of bread, and in prayers. And fear came upon every soul: and many wonders and signs were done by the apostles. And all that believed were together, and had all things common; And sold their possessions and goods, and parted them to all men, as every man had need. And they, continuing daily with one accord in the temple, and breaking bread from house to house, did eat their meat with gladness and singleness of heart, praising God, and having favour with all the people. And the Lord added to the church daily such as should be saved (Acts 2:41–47).

It is clear from these verses they knew exactly what to do from their commissioning. Notice their behavior. The listeners to their teaching received the word, which means the disciples taught Jesus's word—a reference to what He taught them. This was one of the first things they did. They knew to communicate to those who had not been with Jesus. It is clear this was important, because one of the requirements of the disciple who took Judas's place was he had to have been with Jesus (Acts 1:21–26). Why was this so important? How could the twelve, including Matthias, obey the mandate of Matthew 28:18–20 if one of them had not been there to hear what Jesus had taught? This is why the twelve were an official group with a limited number of potential candidates. This is why Paul was an apostle, born out of due time (1 Cor 15:8). Paul had to receive the three-year teaching from Jesus personally, so our Lord met with him in Arabia for three years, as explained in Galatians 1. He also had to see the risen Lord, which occurred on the road to Damascus. Paul had to spend many hours defending his apostleship because many did not know these truths. The apostles were intact with twelve men who had been with Jesus and could have been able to articulate, with the Holy Spirit's help, the truths of our Lord's teaching.

Acts 2 continues with this same mindset. Verse 42 says the followers continued in the apostles' doctrine/teaching. What teaching did they have except that which they had learned from the Lord? Remember, these were unlearned and ignorant men, but the world took notice that they had been with Jesus. Verse 46 confirms they were in the temple daily. The temple was a place of instruction. If you follow the path through Acts, you will see that the temple and synagogues—smaller places of teaching—were the places where the apostles spent their time. They spent their time in these places because they were fulfilling the great commission. Acts 1:8 had already reminded them to go into the entire world. They were seeing Jerusalem filled with the doctrine. Would the world get the same message?

ACTS 3: PETER AND JOHN TOGETHER
IN DISCIPLE-MAKING

Acts 3 has Peter and John, the two men who organized the upper room for the last supper, as the key leaders of the church. Galatians also calls them the pillars of the church (Gal 2:9). They are going to the temple to pray and see what God has for them. It becomes an opportunity to preach Jesus, and this is exactly what Peter did. Acts 4:2 mentions that the religious leaders were upset that Jesus and the resurrection were being preached. It was clear what the disciples were doing. They had been commissioned. Later in chapter 4, Peter and John were rebuked by the religious leaders, and their response is clear, "Whether it be right in the sight of God to hearken unto you more than unto God, judge ye. For we cannot but speak the things which we have seen and heard" (Acts 4:19b–20). Do you see what their response was? They were simply teaching and preaching what they had seen and heard. They had no other message. If only pastors today had the same passion. This was exactly what they have been commissioned to do. Further in chapter 4, they meet together as the leaders of the church and rejoiced that they had been found "worthy" to suffer for Jesus. Then they prayed for boldness to speak Jesus's word (4:29). What word would that be, except what our Lord had given to them? They knew no other word. So they prayed for boldness, and they spoke the word of God with boldness; again, what word?

In Acts 5, the disciples were arrested, and God released them to go and speak in the temple to all the words of this life (Acts 5:20). What words of this life? The words that changed their lives and that could change others as well. When they were caught again, the high priest said that they had filled Jerusalem with their doctrine (Acts 5:28). What teaching? What doctrine? They only knew one Doctrine. They even confirmed that truth by stating they were witnesses of the things that they taught (Acts 5:32). Later in the same chapter they were beaten for preaching the name of Jesus. Acts 5:42 says, "They ceased not to teach and preach Jesus Christ." This had been their commission. They were keeping to this call. They were diligently making converts and communicating to them the details of the commands of Jesus.

ACTS 6: DEACONS' HELP IN DISCIPLE-MAKING

By Acts 6, the disciples were burdened down with the daily ministrations of the call. As a result, the word of God was being neglected. However, by choosing men to assist them, they were able to get back to their calling. It is interesting that they chose men who were full of the Holy Spirit, of honest report, and wise (Acts 6:3). Men like this are called pastors, elders, etc., today. They were investing in the men so much by this time that they were able to have qualified men just to wait on tables. Do we think that the early church came to this level of maturity by accident? This was intentional training. Today I hear pastors and leaders whine about not having qualified men in their church. The early church had qualified men to wait on tables. Do we need to take from their lead?

ACTS 7: STEPHEN HAS BEEN DISCIPLED

In Acts 7, Stephen rehearses the history of Israel all the way to the time of Jesus. Stephen had not been with Jesus and was probably still learning all about the teachings of Jesus. It makes sense that there is little in this chapter on our Lord's teaching. But he closes his teaching with a view of Jesus.

It is important to note that the apostles had been very careful to teach the word of God correctly and efficiently as seen through Jesus.

It has come up time and time again in their teaching. It is also critical that we see they had been a little negligent in the further command of Matthew 28 and Acts 1:8. They were to go into the entire world, and by chapter 7, they were still in Jerusalem. Therefore, chapter 8 introduces us to full-fledged persecution, particularly by one man named Saul. Saul was there at Stephen's death, and he even began to make havoc of the church of Jerusalem (Acts 8:3). As a result, the church was scattered abroad in Acts 8:4, and as they moved about, they began to fulfill the rest of the commission; to go into all the world and preach the gospel—not just in Jerusalem, but into the entire world. And as they went, they preached the word, which undoubtedly would have been the words of Jesus, or just Jesus Himself, because He is the Word (John 1).

ACTS 8: PHILIP BEGAN THE PROCESS

Later in chapter 8, the Lord drew Philip to an Ethiopian. The man was reading from Isaiah 53, but when Philip taught and preached to him, he preached Jesus (Acts 8:35). It is true that Jesus is in Isaiah 53, but I see no reason to doubt that Jesus's life and resurrection were also preached. When finished, the Ethiopian believed that Jesus was the Christ, the Son of God.

ACTS 9: SAUL: THE GREAT DISCIPLE-MAKER IS SAVED

In chapter 9, Saul is saved, and the Lord tells Ananias that Saul is going to be preaching Jesus's name (9:15). The point I am trying to make is that the apostles were determined to preach Jesus, which undoubtedly would have included all that He had taught them, directly fulfilling the Great Commission.

DISCIPLE-MAKERS ALL THROUGH ACTS

As one continues through the book of Acts, one can readily see the theme is clear: preach Jesus. And the disciples did it passionately. The name of Jesus is mentioned at least five times in chapter 9 alone. In chapter 10, the theme continues as such. Acts 10:33 alludes to communicating all the things that have been commanded. Could this be a connection to Matthew 28? Peter adds in Acts 10:42 that he had been commanded to preach unto the people and testify of Jesus. This must be a connection to Matthew 28. Acts 11:26 discloses the apostles were even staying at certain locations for extended periods of time to properly train and disciple the followers. The passion of the Great Commission was becoming embedded into the hearts of those who heard the call of Jesus originally. Acts 12 tells us that the word of God multiplied, and Barnabas and Saul returned from Jerusalem having fulfilled their ministry. What ministry might this be?

In Acts 13, things really began to develop with a strategy to fulfill the Great Commission and the repeated command found in Acts 1:8. The church had fully discovered their requirement to see the truths Jesus taught the twelve were to get out into the entire world. I am sure the loss of some of the original twelve also might have been a motivation. If those who had been with Jesus were dead, could the message have become more difficult to believe? The message must get out, the truth must be told, and time was of the essence. This is why Paul appealed to the existence of more than five hundred brethren who had witnessed the resurrection and were still alive as Jesus taught. Peter called himself an "eyewitness" of Jesus's majesty, drawing direct attention to the Mount of Transfiguration. Therefore, the church prayed and fasted in Acts 13 and called two men who had been identified by the Holy Spirit to go out with the truths.

These two men, Saul (later called Paul) and Barnabas, were to go as the Holy Spirit led and introduce the cities to Jesus. The rest of Acts highlights these three missionary journeys, plus a trip to Rome. The word of the Lord and all that He had commanded was being communicated into the entire world by the apostles and those they had trained. You can see the fulfillment of the Great Commission slowly coming together. But it was not just a commission for the twelve. I believe the command of Matthew 28:18–20 is just as much our responsibility as it was theirs. The question is, will it move out from here or die with us? It concerns me today to see many who are so committed to earthly joys and callings and do not see this passion that must burn in our bosoms. The Great Commission has been relegated to a few and pushed aside as irrelevant far too long. We need a fresh calling to be what our Savior has called us to be. This includes investing our lives into the spiritual nurturing of others. This will take time and will cost us, but do we expect any different from our calling?

If one wanted to do so, one could work his way through the entire book of Acts and watch this attitude and action consistently unfold. The apostles knew they had a mission from God, and they were going to see it through to the end. The gospel entrusted to them had to make it out of

Jerusalem, and it had to be entrusted into the hands of faithful men who would take it and reproduce it in the same way. We are not talking about super Christianity but fundamental Christianity. This is Christianity 101. We have to see that the call of disciple-making is a call that is required of all of us. If your church lacks the godly men to make it happen, start with yourself and lead someone to Christ. Right there you have the foundation for the disciple-making process.

Further in Acts, the church began to ordain elders (14:23). The disciple-making process is being carried to its ultimate end. The result of church leaders, the highest-called position in the world, is now the finished product. I realize that some may not see it this way, but think of it in these terms. What is the major plan that our Lord has to win the world to Himself and prepare the world for His coming? Is it the Jews, the governments, United States of America, or what? It is none of these. His plan is the church, and the gates of hell are not going to prevail against it. Once a man is equipped to lead in the church, he now is in the position of the highest spiritual rank on this earth. There is no higher rank than to be an elder in a church. Remember that the terms elder, pastor, and bishop are all used interchangeably in Scripture (cf., Acts 20:28 and 1 Pet 5:2–4). For someone to become an elder, he has to have this burden put upon him by God. First Timothy 3 mentions a man must aspire to the office of a bishop, elder, or pastor. This desire must come from God, because we are not able to do so in and of ourselves.

Acts 15 reveals how the disciples were teaching and preaching the word of the Lord. They also were beginning to go back to check on the churches they had founded. Why were they going back? They were going back because conversion was not their goal. If conversion was their goal, they would not have needed to go back. They were going back to strengthen the lives of the believers and be sure they were reproducing after their kind. It is expected that believers are to reproduce other believers who are committed and devoted to the cause. We have all been given the mission to make disciples. This includes evangelism and discipleship (leading them to maturity). This is the whole idea Paul expresses in Ephesians 4. The gifted men are to train up others to do the work of the ministry, which is reproducing. It is sad to hear that not only are there believers who have never led anyone to Christ, but there are also those who also have never helped mature a believer. These can no longer be seen as options. We have a mandate from God.

PAUL AND BARNABAS AS DISCIPLE-MAKERS

It is worth noting the exchange between Paul and Barnabas in Acts 15. Paul and Barnabas had been traveling on a missionary journey and leading and discipling others to the Lord. John Mark was also with them, who happened to be the nephew of Barnabas. Earlier in the journey, John Mark apparently left them to return home for reasons unrecorded. He was with them in Acts 12:25 and 13:5, but he left them in Acts 13:13. Barnabas was ready to take his nephew back again with him, but Paul was adamant that he could not go. Nowhere is it recorded exactly why John Mark went home. We can only speculate. For whatever reason, now that he was ready to go with them again, Paul would have none of it. Why? What is the big deal?

The big deal is that we have a mission from God, and we cannot be negligent in this call. Somehow Paul believed that John Mark's departure was inexcusable. There is no room to begin and not finish. Do we not see how seriously they understood the call to make disciples? How dare we take it lightly! On a positive note, you can see at the end of Paul's journey that apparently John Mark was again a proven man, and Paul called for him as he was near the end of his life in 2 Timothy 4:11. There is a place of restoration, but we dare not have to need it. Fight the good fight of faith, and finish well our call.

In the rest of Acts we see the apostles continuing to spread the message, continuing to disciple-make, and continuing to establish churches. The word of God was going forth. They were nearing the end of their time on earth. Many were being martyred, and the process needed to be placed into the hands of faithful men. They did their call well, and as each left this earth to head home, he was able to point to the many who had followed and who had been discipled into the deeper things of God. The church was on the path called by God because they understood their commission from the Lord in Matthew 28. Do we understand our commission?

7

The Epistles Taught It

I count it a privilege to be under the teaching of my pastor, Wally Webster. His great desire to fulfill 2 Timothy 2:2 and raise up men of God is evident to all around him. The three-year Men with a Mission program that Pastor Wally has taught made a huge impact in my life. I had been saved a couple of years when Pastor Wally invited me to take Men with a Mission. At that time, I didn't know a lot about the Scriptures and even less about who I was supposed to be as a servant of the Lord. I graduated from Men with a Mission five years ago and have been growing in the Lord since.

Men with a Mission taught me how to be a servant to my God and to His people, how to be a leader in my home as well as in my church, and how to have a walk that is pleasing to the Lord. There is a lot of emphasis on Scripture memorization in this course. That has been a great asset to me, not only for teaching others, but hiding God's word in my heart has also helped me to live according to His will.

Since I've graduated from Men with a Mission, Pastor Wally has added a fourth class to the program, which is stretching me even further. Praise God. By God's grace, the power of the Holy Spirit, and faithful men like Pastor Wally, I am now teaching others. I have taught from kindergarten through high school and am now involved in teaching Adult Christian Education in my church. Four years ago, I was given the awesome privilege of serving as a deacon in Mount Airy Bible Church. Life is exciting.

I have been truly blessed to have the Men with a Mission program as a vital part of my discipleship process and my sanctification in the Lord.

—Personal testimony of Vance Hunt
Hunt Plumbing and Heating, President
Deacon, Mount Airy Bible Church

IT MAKES SENSE THAT this commissioning made its way into the writings of the apostles. It was their heartbeat, and they followed through masterfully. They modeled it in their writings and explicitly taught the process. It is fascinating to observe.

DISCIPLE-MAKING IN ROMANS

First, apostles modeled disciple-making. Our Lord made it clear the apostles were to invest in other men (Matt 28:18–21). Jesus did it for them. Jesus sent them out in pairs. Jesus worked on them one-on-one and in small-group situations. Jesus gave individuals and pairs specific tasks. He was committed to investing in the men so they could invest in others. The apostles clearly picked up on this. Few examples show the apostles acting by themselves. They were given a mission—notice this mission in the introduction of their writings. The book of Romans begins with Paul's name alone, but there is Romans 16:22 in which Tertius is added as the copier of the epistle. Tertius must have been there with him. Why? Was Paul unable to write because an eye problem, or shackles, or age? We can only speculate. Regardless, Tertius is there with him. What is Paul doing with Tertius? Is Paul not investing into his life?

DISCIPLE-MAKING IN 1 CORINTHIANS

Paul begins 1 Corinthians with these words, "Paul, called to be an apostle of Jesus Christ through the will of God, and Sosthenes our brother." Paul included someone else in his writings. Who is Sosthenes? Acts 18:17 describes him as the chief ruler of the synagogue. There had to be a reason Sosthenes was beaten. The only reason recorded in Scripture that people were beaten in that day was because of their faith. It seems Sosthenes had come to faith, and Paul was probably discipling him. Then Paul includes him as he writes back to Corinth, the hometown of Sosthenes. Paul is writing to Corinth from Ephesus, which would mean Sosthenes went with Paul. Why? So Paul could invest further into his life.

DISCIPLE-MAKING IN 2 CORINTHIANS

Second Corinthians begins, "Paul, an apostle of Jesus Christ by the will of God, and Timothy our brother . . ." We know the history of Timothy better. Paul later wrote two books to him because Timothy had taken on the role of shepherding, just as Paul would have invested in him to do. We will look closer at Timothy when we get to those books, but for now we see another man in whom Paul is personally investing time to train up for the work of the Lord. Paul realized his time was short. He had already suffered much at the hands of the enemy, and it would only be a matter of time before he would die. What would happen to that which our Lord had personally invested into him? Would it die with him? Not hardly. Paul was serious about his Great Commission.

DISCIPLE-MAKING IN PHILIPPIANS AND COLOSSIANS

We see Paul and Timothy together again as Paul writes in Philippians and Colossians. Is it possible that Timothy was regularly with Paul while he was in prison? Philippians and Colossians are what we call prison epistles, which means they were written from prison. Timothy must have been with him for Paul to include him in the introduction as he did. Paul was probably doing several things by having him there. First, Paul was probably investing into Timothy's life, and second, he was validating Timothy to audiences who would later need Timothy's input. Timothy was part of the next generation to come forward, especially being younger than Paul (1 Tim 4:12). Paul saw it as his personal responsibility to train others to take his place. I believe with all my heart that every believer needs to have this same passion. Paul said if you want to follow Christ, follow me. It is this simple, and we dare not overlook our calling.

DISCIPLE-MAKING IN 1 AND 2 THESSALONIANS

In 1 and 2 Thessalonians, Paul mentions Timothy and Silvanus. Silvanus is another spelling for Silas, a man who was often with Paul on his missionary journeys. Paul took Silas with him after Paul and Barnabas had their falling out regarding John Mark. Silas became a prominent person who spent many hours with Paul. Again, what is Paul doing? Is Paul lonely and afraid? Does Paul need someone to tuck him in at night? No. Paul is committed to doing the Great Commission. Are we?

DISCIPLE-MAKING IN 1 AND 2 TIMOTHY

First and Second Timothy and Titus are called the Pastoral Epistles. They get this name because Paul wrote to them as they were pastoring churches. We may not be sure how much time Paul had personally invested into Titus, but Timothy was like his own son in the faith. Regardless, Paul is using precious investment time to pour into these men to write to them and set things in order for the proper calling of the ministry. He even gives them the specifics of the calling of elders. Notice Luke is with Paul near the end of 2 Timothy. Here is another man Paul is investing into and Luke, of course, writes the book of Luke.

I want to focus on one specific verse in 2 Timothy. It is my theme verse for the men's ministry at our church, and it ought to be every church's theme verse for their men's ministry. Second Timothy 2:2 precisely defines the plan, "And the things that thou hast heard of me among many witnesses, the same commit thou to faithful men, who shall be able to teach others also" (2 Tim 2:2). This is the Pauline version of the Great Commission. It is amazing how Matthew 28:19–20 and 2 Timothy 2:2 parallel. Both talk about disciple-making in its purest sense. We have several generations of Great Commission progress. Paul received it directly from the Lord (Gal 1). Paul passed it on to Timothy, as shown throughout Acts and the Epistles. Timothy is challenged to find faithful men to invest in, so they can in turn teach others. This is how we have it today. Faithful men came along and were taught by those who had been taught, and the rest is history. Of course, the future is still up for grabs. In other words, will there be faithful men in our lives who we are going to invest in, and will they in turn pass it on? They will if we do our part in finding faithful men. And we know our Lord has promised to build His church, so the future of the church is bright. Nevertheless, each of us must take this responsibility and do what we know is required of us. It will only happen if we are yielded unreservedly to His will and call for our lives.

DISCIPLE-MAKING IN PHILEMON

In the book of Philemon, we see an example of Paul investing in several men. He meets Onesimus in prison, leads him to Christ, and then disciples him in some manner regarding obedience and the right way to respond to his position of slavery. Paul then pens a letter to Philemon, who he had probably also led to Christ and discipled (Phil 19), and reminds Philemon of how he ought to act in such circumstances. What an example of taking both men's maturity to another level.

DISCIPLE-MAKING IN 1 PETER

Peter includes Silvanus and Mark in the last chapter of 1 Peter. Apparently these two are with him as well. These men are not concerned about who gets the glory for something. They are so committed to making sure that the Gospel message is carried out that they don't mind sharing brethren. There is a higher calling than a personal agenda. Later we see John mention an elder named Gaius. He seems to be personally investing in him. It is clear just from the headings, introductions, and name connections that the early church apostles saw the need to invest in others to continue what our Lord had started.

8

Paul to Timothy

It may be hard to believe, but my first impression of the importance of devotion to God and our Christian faith was as a first grader in public school only a few miles from our nation's capitol. The teachers and principal led each morning singing with us "*My Country 'Tis of Thee*" (of Jesus Christ), followed by the *Lord's Prayer*. The only minor controversy was whether the *Lord's Prayer* was said, "*Forgive our trespassers*" or "*forgive our debtors.*" In the interest of tolerance, it was explained that either way was acceptable, but that the school had to choose one way to say it, so we said, "*Forgiving our trespassers.*"

This was followed later in the public school year by our favorite Christmas carols and Christmas pageants during the Christmas season. Around Easter, we would practice singing more Christian songs for the Easter season pageant put on for the parents. Diversity included singing African American *spirituals* and learning how Christmas and Easter were celebrated in Latin America.

Then one day in the early 1960s while we were studying American history, the school principal announced that the United States Supreme Court had banned the Lord's Prayer. Just a few years after this, my memories of teachers who were the authority figures leading us in the *Lord's Prayer* each day were contrasted with teachers dressed as hippies and teaching counterculture, which did not include mention of God or our Christian faith, at least not in a positive light.

Being brought up early on with such a universal belief in the importance of God, Jesus, and our Christian faith, I wanted the same for my children. After careful searching, we came to Pastor Wally's church. I soon became shocked that after nearly fifty years of church attendance and Bible study, most church members and many children knew much more of the Bible and the tenants of our Christian faith than I did.

I immediately enrolled in the pastor's Men with a Mission classes and began to learn the basic teachings that were somehow missed during a lifetime of church attendance and wanting to be a good Christian husband and father. Just a sampling of missed teachings is that Jesus is not just *a way,* but the *only way.* Salvation is not by *works,* but by *grace* as a free gift. There is the *evil one* at work in the world today, and the way to make the *evil one* flee is to repeat the *word* of God as Jesus did. Jesus wants us to lead a holy life and to disregard the ways of the world when these are in conflict with the Bible.

Better late than never. Hopefully other men can benefit from Men with a Mission classes too!

—Personal testimony of Greg Jones
Engineering Supervisor, Office of Transportation Engineering
Public Works Division, Frederick County Government

I WANT TO SHOW you a few examples of New Testament men and trace their development through the New Testament, at least as much as we can ascertain from the text. We will examine Timothy, Epaphras, Epaphroditus, Apollos, Artemis, Tychicus, Zenas, and Erastus. Now, not all of these are household names. Some are merely mentioned in the New Testament and some are not even discussed throughout the teaching of church leadership. However, each of these men had a role in having the faith passed on to us today. They seemed to understand the Great Commission was not an option. They seemed to understand the message would die if they did not get this message out. They were not going to allow it to happen on their watch. Do we take it to this level of passion?

TIMOTHY AS A DISCIPLE

Our first example is Timothy. We are introduced to Timothy in Acts 16:1. Paul calls Timothy "my own son in the faith" (1 Tim 1:2). Is this because Paul had actually led him to Christ or that he personally took Timothy under his wing and led him toward maturity? Either way, Paul was greatly instrumental in Timothy's maturity. If Timothy came to Christ through his own godly mother and grandmother, which is rather possible, then Paul calling Timothy a son is directly connected to the maturing process. This would suggest a far greater importance of discipleship.

In Acts 16:1, Timothy is called a certain disciple. By this time, he is already on the way to becoming a serious follower of Jesus. The verse goes on to state that his mother was a Jewess who believed and his father was a Greek (that his father did not believe is implied by the absence). We also see his father's faith is left out in 2 Timothy 1:5. Maybe Paul took on the spiritual father role to Timothy, who had no believing father? Acts 16:2 further adds that Timothy was "well reported of by the brethren that were at Lystra and Iconium" (Acts 16:2). Timothy was becoming a man of prominence even before Paul was discipling him. Remember, Paul said we were to look for faithful men, not just warm bodies. Timothy was someone to whom Paul could entrust the sacred truths of Jesus and know they would be passed on to the next generation. Paul was becoming Paul the Aged, and he needed someone in which to pour the things he had been taught. This was discipleship at its highest peak. Although starting churches and evangelism are important, the necessity of entrusting these babes in Christ into trustworthy hands cannot be underestimated. This is why, in part, Paul emphasized the need to ordain elders in every city. The many new believers needed proper direction, and with all the schisms and false teachers during this time, sound doctrine and leadership could not be overlooked.

Acts 16:3 shows the importance Paul saw in Timothy. It says, "Him (Timothy) would Paul have to go forth with him" (Acts 16:3). Was Paul lonely? Was Paul incompetent? Was Paul afraid? No. This was the call of the disciple-maker, and Paul knew the importance of investing into a "son in the faith." Many pastors today appear more like the Lone Ranger than the apostle Paul. Pastors often work long hours, visit many homes and hospitals, and invest in the care of the church. They are to be commended for their compassion, but not their wisdom. After leading a church for many years, they die, and the church is left in disarray. Why? No one was trained to take over the ministry. No pastor should do a visit without taking along a Timothy. I realize in some circumstances, it is not possible; however, every pastor needs a list of men, their emergency numbers, and a way to contact them in any situation. I have yet to ask a man to go to a hospital, funeral home, etc., when he has not been more than willing. I have had the opportunity to take many brothers on visits, and now they are doing this work better than I could ever imagine. It is self-centered pride that keeps us from taking men and investing in them. What are we afraid of? Are we afraid people may like them better than us, want them to preach over us, or desire to be with them more than us? If this happens, humbly give them the lead and find another person to serve. The fields are white unto harvest.

I remember one day in my office a parishioner was chastising me about another "leader" in the church and how I needed to be careful. As I probed further, he stated to me that if I wasn't careful, this other leader was going to split the church and take many with him. I calmly responded, "Let him take them." The church is bigger than me or him. If he wants to split the church and take these families, more power to him. I then dismissed the man and left the office with the joy of the Lord. Both the man in my office and this so-called leader left shortly after that, and no one went with them. Even the man in the office did not follow the so-called leader. We pastors need to get over ourselves if we feel threatened. Train up men to take over the ministry, let them do it, and get out of the way. We should have given up our pride the day we surrendered to Jesus. God resists the proud and hates pride. Get over it, and let the Lord have His way with His church.

SILAS ENABLES TIMOTHY

In Acts 17:14, Paul seems to have been separated for a short while from Timothy, and Paul left him in the hands of Silas. But in verse 15, just one verse later, Paul commands Silas and Timothy to come to him with all speed. In both verses, Silas is mentioned ahead of Timothy. Is it possible for a while that Silas was part of the disciple-making process to Timothy? Remember, our ultimate goal is not to be the one to personally train, but see that it gets done. There is no limit to what could happen if no one cared who got the credit for the results. God has chosen who He has chosen. He has called them in such a way so that no flesh can glory in His presence. In Acts 18:5, Silas and Timothy catch up with Paul. Now there are two who Paul is entrusting with the many unsearchable riches of God.

TIMOTHY AND ERASTUS

After Paul passed through Macedonia and Achaia, he sent into Macedonia two of those who ministered unto him, Timothy and Erastus. We will look at Erastus a little later, but for now, we see once again Paul investing in Timothy. We see him actually modeling the Lord Jesus, as Jesus Himself earlier had sent out the disciples in pairs to do the work of the ministry

(Mark 6:7). You can be sure this was part of the training of Timothy. Once we get to Acts 20:4, Timothy is listed among others who are accompanying Paul. It is clear that whenever Paul sent him out, he was expected to return with a report. Paul was duplicating his ministry all over the world, just as Jesus commanded. I am sure the command of Matthew 28 was reinforced to Paul in Arabia by our Lord. It was too critical of a commandment to let it fall on deaf ears.

TIMOTHY IN ROMANS AND 1 CORINTHIANS

Paul includes Timothy at the end of Romans 16 as one of those who wants to greet the Romans. Is it possible that Timothy had been to Rome with Paul? Paul calls Timothy "my workfellow." Timothy was proving trustworthy to Paul as he was nearing the end of his calling.

Of all the verses including Timothy, none are clearer than 1 Corinthians 4:17, "For this cause have I sent unto you Timotheus, who is my beloved son and faithful in the Lord, who shall bring you into remembrance of my ways which be in Christ, as I teach everywhere in every church" (1 Cor 4:17). This is exactly what Paul has been modeling, teaching, and living since his call to the ministry. He was looking for faithful men to entrust with these truths. How can we, as pastors, miss this calling? Do we only need to have a fishing buddy, golfing buddy, or weightlifting partner? We are talking about the call of God and the Scriptures. If you, as a pastor, have been entrusted with these truths from some faithful men, then you have this call upon you. We better take it seriously.

Paul calls Timothy "faithful," the same word as "faithful" in 2 Timothy 2:2, and is confident Timothy is going to remember the things Paul has taught him. Paul knew the importance of this process, and he passed it on to Timothy, his son in the faith. In 2 Corinthians 1:19, Paul includes Timothy as one who had preached to Corinth. Not only did Paul disciple Timothy, but he must also have put him through a class on expository preaching. Apparently Paul had given Timothy the pulpit to present the truths he was learning. I can only imagine the process of Paul helping Timothy step-by-step with exegesis, discovery, and presentation. Then I imagine the two of them discussing the results of the message over a bagel! Paul was later going to give a full-time pulpit to Timothy. He was not going to do so without preparing Timothy for the calling.

TIMOTHY IN PHILIPPIANS

There is probably not enough time or paper available to fully deal with the magnitude of Philippians 2:19–23. It is imperative to review the entire passage.

> But I trust in the Lord Jesus to send Timotheus shortly unto you, that I also may be of good comfort, when I know your state. For I have no man likeminded, who will naturally care for your state. For all seek their own, not the things which are Jesus Christ's. But ye know the proof of him, that, as a son with the father, he hath served with me in the gospel. Him therefore I hope to send presently, so soon as I shall see how it will go with me (Phil 2:19–23).

Paul had a special fondness for the Philippians. The start of this church was very dear to him. It was his first encounter in Macedonia, and this church was birthed in blood and tears. He had been beaten and left in prison after seeing several wonderful conversions. Acts 16 goes on to describe the jail cell doors being opened and the jailer preparing to kill himself. He then cries out to Paul, "What must I do to be saved?" Some have thought he was referring to saving his neck. When a prisoner escaped under your watch, you were to die. But it is important to note that Paul had already told him they were all still there and none had escaped. He was not asking for physical salvation, but spiritual salvation. What must I do to obtain eternal life? He had heard Paul praying, singing, and rejoicing after a beating. He had something they did not have. He wanted it. Paul then led him to Christ, as well as the jailer's whole family. The Philippian church was born.

With this in mind, Paul is writing to the Philippians while once again being in prison (1:13). I am sure his newest prison experience was driving his thoughts to the prison experience at Philippi. He also knew the Philippians needed a shepherd. Who does Paul pick? On the top of the list of candidates is his son Timothy. He was not going to entrust this dear church into the hands of just anyone. It was going to take a special man of God. The answer was clear: Timothy.

Paul goes on to explain more things about Timothy. He had already included him in the introduction (1:1). He was going to explain more about this man to them. In 2:19, he says he trusted in the Lord to send Timothy to them. Paul was confident in what the Lord was doing in him and had observed such fruit. Paul then goes on to say he has no likeminded man who will naturally care for them. What a quality Timothy had. He naturally cared for others. Paul said he had no one like him on his whole list. Had Timothy learned from his mother and grandmother? I am sure they must have had some part in this. And so did Paul. Did he not naturally care for others? Paul earlier mentioned his willingness to be accursed for his lost friends (Rom 9:3). In Philippians 1, he mentioned his desire to go and be with Christ, but "to abide in the flesh is more needful for you" (Phil 1:24). He would rather give his life to others than seek selfish pleasure. Oh if this were pastors' passion today! Too many are using the calling to get for themselves. Even the Son of Man came not to be ministered unto, but to minister, and to give His life a ransom for many. Jesus modeled sacrificial living. How can we as pastors live any other way?

Paul continues in Philippians saying they had proof that Timothy had served with Paul in the gospel. He was acting as a son with a father. This is close companionship. Timothy is the learner under the father-teacher, Paul. The Philippians were going to be recipients of this investment.

TIMOTHY IN 1 THESSALONIANS

Another chapter from Paul that includes Timothy is 1 Thessalonians. In chapter 3, Paul mentions his "worry" over the Thessalonians. When he could no longer forebear, he sent Timothy to establish them. He calls Timothy "our brother and minister of God, and our fellowlabourer in the gospel of Christ" (1 Thess 3:2). One can clearly see he has high regard for Timothy. The Thessalonians needed to have their faith strengthened. Timothy was the man. Throughout this chapter, Paul writes using "we." The "we" seems to be those in his introduction, including Silvanus and Timothy. In chapter 3, he mentions the influence these men had on the Thessalonians. Verse 4 says, "We told you . . ." In verse 5, he says again he could no longer forebear; he had to know about their faith. Paul realized the conversion of the Thessalonians was not the ultimate call. We have somehow placed evangelism at a higher level than even stated in Scripture. Jesus did not, in the Great Commission, say go out and make converts. He said go out and make disciples. They are not the same thing. Paul had many converts at Thessalonica, as discovered in Acts 17:1–10. But his worry in 1 Thessalonians 3:5 was clear, "For this cause, when I could no longer forebear, I sent to know your faith, lest by some means the tempter have tempted you, and our labour be in vain." Did Paul not know whether they were saved? It's doubtful. His concern was the Great Commission. Salvation was only part of the calling. For his labor to be in vain, it would mean the Great Commission was not moving from Thessalonica. This was his labor—entrust to faithful men. He wanted to be sure the gospel spread beyond him.

Paul received the news as stated in the next verse. Timothy came back and brought to Paul good tidings of their faith. What was it about their faith that Timothy brought back to Paul? Acts 17 states that Paul only spent a few weeks in Thessalonica, which would mean he hardly had time to invest in them. Because of safety concerns, he had to flee. In the meantime, he was praying night and day exceedingly that we (notice the plural) might see their face (it had been a while since he had been there), and perfect that which is lacking in their faith (1 Thess 3:10). What was lacking in their faith? He had already mentioned their salvation faith in chapter 1, when he says they are, "followers of us, and of the Lord" (1 Thess 1:6), and he says they had turned to God from idols and were serving the living and true God. In 2:13 Paul says they had received the word of God as truth, and in verse 19 of the same chapter, he discusses the hope of seeing them in the presence of the Lord. There is no question Paul was convinced these believers had saving faith. What could be lacking in their faith? We have to remember Paul had only been at this church for several weeks. This was hardly enough time to disciple the believers to maturity. He needed more time with them. They were lacking maturity in their faith. The word for "perfect" in the King James Version is the same root word as in Ephesians 4:12. Paul was desirous to mature the saints. This is what was lacking in their faith.

This is exactly what I believe is lacking in many believers' faith today. We have churches full of converts, or professing converts, and we wonder why there are such troubles, splits, and problems. There are at least two clear reasons. First, we are trying to sanctify the dead. We are trying to push, exhort, challenge, and encourage many other spiritual efforts toward the dead in trespasses and sins, and we are accomplishing little. We cannot get a pulse from some in the church community because there has never been true regeneration. We struggle with those who profess faith and have little or no fruit. We need to stop trying to breathe energy into these folks, and instead introduce them to the Savior. Good works are a natural outgrowth of those truly in Christ. James 2 makes this clear. No fruit or good works strongly suggests there is no salvation. We need to stop trying to sanctify that which has never been regenerated.

Second, there might be those who are lacking in the faith today because they have never been properly discipled. Coming to church week after week, regardless of how many services you might have, is not the same as disciple-making. Attending small groups, being in a Bible study, or listening to tapes or Christian radio are good things, but do not guarantee a disciple. Ephesians 4 teaches an intentional process, not a general path, to this result. Jesus had invested into Paul. Paul invested into Timothy, as well as many others. Paul was expecting Timothy to invest in the Thessalonians, a desire Paul had for himself, but had been hindered from doing so (1 Thess 2:18). Yet Paul continued to pray toward this end. Now Timothy, Paul's son in the faith, was going to mature them in the manner that Paul was not able to do. Remember, Paul was more interested in their growth than who was actually doing the work. If we pastors had such a passion for our people, then we too should not be concerned about who is doing the work. It is all the work of God. As Paul has recorded for us in Philippians 1:15–16, "Some indeed preach Christ even of envy and strife; and some also of good will: The one preach Christ of contention, not sincerely, supposing to add affliction to my bonds."

TIMOTHY IN HEBREWS

There is one more example outside of 1 and 2 Timothy that we will examine next. The writer of Hebrews (whoever this man was) said Timothy might come to them shortly. I am not sure what the intent was, but these Hebrew Christians surely had some mixed-up theology. The writer had exhorted them to go on to maturity and leave the elementary principles behind (Heb 6:1). It is interesting that the same word for maturity in Ephesians 4 is found in Hebrews 13, just two verses ahead of the mentioning of Timothy.

> Now the God of peace, that brought again from the dead our Lord Jesus, that great shepherd of the sheep, through the blood of the everlasting covenant, Make you perfect in every good work to do his will, working in you that which is wellpleasing in his sight, through Jesus Christ; to whom be glory for ever and ever. Amen (Heb 13:20–21).

It seems plausible Timothy was going to be part of this maturing process, which, to Paul, was paramount for true faith.

9

1 and 2 Timothy Disciples

On July 31, 1996, I received a letter from my pastor that changed my life. It was an invitation to join Men with a Mission and be challenged to grow deeper in my commitment to the Lord Jesus. In the letter, Pastor Wally said he desired to be faithful to the Scriptures—2 Timothy 2:2 and Ephesians 4:11–14—and was looking for some faithful men.

Throughout this three-year study, Pastor challenged us to "raise the bar." Meeting regularly with other men who loved and were committed to Jesus provided positive peer pressure. We learned many things, like what a disciple is, how to study the Bible, how to develop a life of purity, how to share our faith, and how to pray. We learned about fasting, servanthood, hermeneutics, and marriage issues, just to name a few, and we memorized many verses of Scripture.

When I started the program, I was a newly committed follower of Christ and had no vision for what God desired to do in my life. With this program, Pastor Wally developed in me a genuine love for the study of the Scriptures and whetted my appetite for more formal education. Seven years after graduating from the Men with a Mission program, I graduated from Southern Evangelical Seminary and now lead our Adult Christian Education Ministry. This would have not happened apart from the commitment of my pastor, the Men with a Mission program, and the grace of God. To God be the glory.

—Personal testimony of Steve Schrader
Patton Electronics, Vice-President of Manufacturing

IT WOULD BE IMPOSSIBLE to complete a study of Timothy without an examination of the two epistles that bear his name. Paul wrote two letters, that we know of, to his son in the faith Timothy. Numerous facts should be noted in these two books:

1. 1 Timothy 1:1: Paul is an apostle by the commandment of Jesus. To which commandment is Paul referring? Is it possible that the commandment is describing the manner of his apostleship, more than the actual call? I am this kind of disciple-making apostle—this is what Jesus commanded me to do. In addition, all of us have been commanded to make disciples according to Matthew 28.

2. 1 Timothy 1:3: Paul challenges Timothy to charge them to teach no other doctrine. Apparently Timothy already had others teaching for him. Was this not the process of 2 Timothy 2:2?

3. 1 Timothy 1:18–20: Paul mentions the charge that he committed to Timothy. What charge was this? I believe the next verse answers this question as Paul uses several examples of those who had "put away concerning faith have made shipwreck" (1:19). This was not the original charge. The charge was to persevere. Disciple-making was not complete until those we had entrusted were doing the same with what they had been entrusted.

4. In chapter 3, Paul lists the qualifications for men to be the leaders in the church. This list refers to the pastors, bishops, and elders of the local church. This is not a work on church polity, but it is clear from the Greek these terms are used interchangeably (1 Pet 5, Acts 20). These are not three different leaders. This list and others refer to the pastor leaders of the local church. Not only were Paul and Timothy involved in training up faithful men, but they were also alerted to ordain elders to do the work of the leadership of the ministry. This was a list for them to measure the qualified leaders against the "wannabes." Every church has those who aspire to leadership for all the wrong reasons. Leadership training must be prayerfully developed. Putting a man in leadership is a very serious action. Once you have him in this position, it is nearly impossible, short of tragic death, to move him out. This is why Scripture warns to not lay hands too quickly on a leader (1 Tim 5:22). Leadership must be carefully examined, prayed over, and discerned. Better to be too slow than to be too hasty. We have a plan that takes approximately five years for a man to become

an elder. There are specific safeguards in place to watch over the man before he is given a leadership position. You cannot be too careful in this area. Train up men, and realize not all men will become an elder.

5. Chapter 4 warns of those who are going to depart from the faith. This also is a caution to be careful and watch for this attitude in the leadership area. If a man is placed in leadership too early and departs from the faith, it will cause much damage. It will cause damage to those who placed such a man in leadership. Although we often fall short in this process, we don't want to have a track record of poor choices in leadership.

6. Chapter 5 gives more specific details about elder rule, women's ministry, and widows. There are cautions on how to approach an elder, how to deal with a sinning elder, and to pay an elder. Again, remember that we are talking about pastors, elders, bishops, shepherds, ministers, or whatever name is preferred. There are specific guidelines to protect the leadership and hold them accountable. Spiritual leaders need accountability and to be held accountable. No spiritual leader is above confrontation, but it must be done biblically. I am reminded of the fear that godly David felt in approaching godless Saul in the Old Testament. I believe that parishioners and others need to be cautious about approaching a man of God. Yet, it still needs to be done and should be. Pastors are just one of a group of leaders in the church. Pastors need to lead their leaders with the fear of God in their hearts. Lead, but do not drive them. Be a team. These are men you are investing in to lead in the church you have been called to shepherd. These men ought to be the first men you invest in to mature. Do not assume they are walking with God. Teach, train, and shepherd them, and then help them catch the vision of Matthew 28. Do not assume they fully understand this passion until they have caught it and are living it.

7. In chapter 6, Paul concludes with a great exhortation to Timothy to fight the good fight of faith. In other words, there are going to be times and cause to quit. The faith is not about a season or epoch of one's life. We are in this to the finish, and this is the message that must be taught to all believers. We have those who

say they have paid their dues. I have heard this often from older saints who won't serve. Instead, the young moms who need to be in worship, etc., are called to work in nurseries, etc. Yet, it is these same young moms who miss services for sick children and other related pressures of early parenting.

There is no retirement in the call of God. Timothy, fight the good fight of faith. Pastors, there is no retirement. Elders, there is no quitting. Finish well. Finish as fathers, grandfathers, and patriarchs. Where are quitting, retirement, and leaving part of the call of God? Disciple-making is a lifelong process. What great leaders of the church are spending most of their days with their feet in the sand, their hands on a putter or fishing rod, or traveling all over? What a shame to the call of God. No wonder some believers are going to be ashamed at His appearing. When God called us to follow Him, there was no time constraint. We were purchased by His blood, and this is for a lifetime commitment. Sad that so many see it only as a convenience issue for them. If you have chosen this self-centered retirement life, find a good local church, sit down with the pastor, and ask him to use you to the fullest. You will be the more blessed for it.

8. Second Timothy continues the same themes that are presented in 1 Timothy. In chapter 1, Paul challenges Timothy about his lineage. Notice in verse 3 that Paul mentions he serves God from his forefathers. It is important to remember that Paul was a first-generation Christian. There is no evidence that his personal forefathers ever believed. He is talking about those who had invested into his life and the call of the church. These forefathers have given to us, and we need to understand that it must be passed on to those who follow. The next verse mentions the passion Paul had, with his desire to invest in others.

9. Second Timothy 1:9 reminds us we have been saved "according to His own purpose." We were saved neither because of our works nor for our agenda. We need to be sure that we understand the call of God on our lives, and just do it. Nike has had the slogan for years, but it is really the heart of the New Testament. Stop talking about it and just do it! Our churches talk about prayer and never do it. We talk of holding a revival, but maybe we better

let one loose. We talk of being a New Testament church and yet we do not have an intentional disciple-making program in place. How can we call ourselves a New Testament church without one? The early church had one, lived it out, and we are the fruit of their investment. What if they had kept it only to themselves? Where would we be today? The disciple-making process lies in our laps now. Because you are reading this book, you are more accountable. What will you do with it?

10. Second Timothy 2 is the most important chapter on this subject because Paul does not just discuss it in theory; he lays out the exact process. In verse 1, Paul calls Timothy his son. This has already been discussed, as Paul is the spiritual mentor to Timothy. Then Paul goes on to explain the disciple-making process. "And the things that thou hast heard of me among many witnesses, the same commit thou to faithful men who shall be able to teach others also" (2 Tim 2:2). Paul had taught Timothy, and he expected Timothy to commit himself (this is the cost) to faithful men who would be able to teach others also. This is what disciple-making really is. We are committing ourselves to faithful men. It will cost many hours, many tears, and many days of investment. It is the disciple-making call. This is also one reason why many pastors do not commit to disciple-making. They are not willing to pay the price.

This is why Jesus called His followers to surrender and consider the cost. If you are not willing to pay the price, don't make the decision to follow. The church can no longer cater to the world and duplicate itself on the altar of ease. Jesus preached a cost. Paul preached a cost. The early church understood the cost. It has not changed biblically, but it has changed in the mind of many who choose to follow. We need to go back to the basics of the call. Paul continues to develop this theme in the rest of the chapter. He uses the illustrations of soldiers, athletes, and farmers. In other words, this call of disciple-making is hard work and labor. We often study 2 Timothy 2:3–10 as separate from 2 Timothy 2:2. This is an unfortunate break in the English. Verse 3 begins with "Thou therefore," which means, "in light of what I just said." Then he goes on to develop the theme of verses 3–10. Notice all the intense words in this section: endure hardness, soldier, warreth, strive, laboreth, suffer, bonds, and endure. Paul is making it clear that disciple-making (2:2) is not an easy task. But it is our call. We need to stop investing in things of the church that distract us from doing the call of God.

11. Second Timothy also adds the classic verse about the importance of studying the Scriptures so we are not ashamed, but rightly dividing the word of truth. If pastors spent more time in the word and less watching movies for a relevant clip or reading secular materials to be current with the time, we would be more relevant to our culture. God's word needs no help. It is quick and powerful and can produce fruit with its Holy Spirit pages. How sad that pastors have been duped into believing that our generation cannot handle the exegetical teaching and preaching of Scripture. We have been told we have to touch all senses, we have to be relevant, and we have to cater to them so they are not offended and gradually bring them into the light. We have also been told people today cannot sit and listen to preaching for more than twenty to thirty minutes. Maybe this is why Paul called it the "foolishness of preaching." Preach the word, dear pastor, and watch God work.

    A man one day came to John Wesley and said no one was coming to hear him preach. Wesley told him, "Catch on fire with enthusiasm and people will come for miles to watch you burn."[1] Oh, how we need the fire back in the pulpit. You cannot get it from Wall Street, Main Street, or Sesame Street. It is found in the precious pages of Holy Writ. Paul then says we are to "shun profane and vain babblings." Maybe he was listening to modern-day preachers! Preach the word.

12. Later in this same chapter, Paul reminds Timothy to be the servant of the Lord and to teach—instructing others. This repeats the same premise Paul has been postulating all through his teaching. All of us are teachers. All of us can teach. We all do not have the gift of teaching. So formal teaching might not be our forte, but this does not preclude us from teaching. Teaching is the key to the disciple-making process. This is why Jesus called all of His

1. Wesley.

followers to be teachers (Matt 28:19–20). Teach what you have been taught so that you in turn can teach others. It is disciple-making at its best.

13. Chapter 3 reminds the reader of the sad departure the professing community is going to take. I believe this chapter does not diagnose the world but the professing community. The world has always been lovers of their own selves, covetous, etc. We only have hope, away from these sins, by coming to Christ. It is sad that as things get near the end, the professing community is going to so resemble the world that you will struggle to distinguish them. The wheat and the tares will be so intermingled, the true profession and false profession will be hard to determine because the true believers will use some of those in the professing community as reasons to live in sinful behavior. Today all of the sinful practices mentioned in chapter 3 can be found in some professing communities as legitimate. It all begins with men loving themselves. The self-esteem movement has been so sold to the Christian community that you can hardly read a book, hear a message, or listen to a speaker without them exhorting us to have a better self-esteem. If we understand the call of God to die to self, is this not a call in the opposite direction? Disciple-making gets to the core of this ideal. We are not our own. We do not need a better self-esteem, but instead a better view that we are just clay pots (2 Cor 4:7). Our worth comes not in the fact that we are who we are, but in the grand view that God has poured His value into that which is otherwise valueless. I can only imagine Jesus sitting down with Peter and trying to get him to improve his self-esteem so that he will not stick his foot in his mouth so often. What Peter needed was not to esteem self, but to die to self. This is disciple-making, and we cannot help but produce this in those we disciple if it is not part of who we are. The call is clear.

14. Chapter 3 adds once again the importance of the curriculum that we must have in our disciple-making process—the Scriptures. These verses are extremely valuable in our understanding of this process. Let me share them in their entirety.

> But evil men and seducers shall wax worse and worse, deceiving, and being deceived. But continue thou in the things which

thou hast learned and hast been assured of, knowing of whom
thou hast learned them; and that from a child thou hast known
the holy scriptures, which are able to make thee wise unto salvation through faith which is in Christ Jesus. All scripture is
given by inspiration of God, and is profitable for doctrine, for
reproof, for correction, for instruction in righteousness: That
the man of God may be perfect, thoroughly furnished unto all
good works (2 Tim 3:13–17).

There is so much here to enjoy about the entire disciple-making
process. In verse 14, Paul tells Timothy to continue in the things
he has learned; including not only the doctrine, but also the
process of getting this teaching into the hands of others. Verse
14 adds that Timothy is to be mindful of those who have taught
him, "Knowing of whom thou hast learned them." Be mindful of
the fact there are faithful men who studied and learned and are
now investing into you. This keeps one in perspective regarding
the importance of investment. Others spent hours growing and
maturing, and now they are willing to invest in you. Take this
process seriously. Timothy was on this pace since he was a child.
This also lends further support to the fact Paul did not lead
Timothy to Christ, but Timothy was already a believer when he
caught up with Paul. For Paul to call him "his son in the faith,"
there might be a connection to the disciple-making process. In
other words, making disciples, not converts, is the goal. Verse
16 adds the four-fold description of the importance of Scripture
and verse 17 again mentions that maturity comes through these
Scriptures. This is God's curriculum.

15. Chapter 4 closes with many exhortations about the process. Verse
    2 hits on all the major components of discipleship. There is the
    word, the reproving, the rebuking, and whatever else is necessary
    to see a believer mature.

16. Paul added that he was ready to leave this earth because he had
    kept the faith. What does this mean? It means he had kept the faith
    moving, because he had invested in those who would guarantee
    the faith would move on to others. Others would be assured of a
    chance to know Christ because Paul had given his best to see that
    others would have this opportunity. He then goes on to mention

a list of names of people who had been a part of this process. In verse 11 he includes Mark, the earlier one who had forsaken him. He was profitable as one who could carry on the task for others. Paul said, "He is profitable to me for the ministry" (2 Tim 4:11). It is always about the ministry, which is giving out the message and seeing that it can move on to the next generation. It is investing in the lives of others, or as I have called it, disciple-making. Paul was content to die, knowing that the call of our Lord to him personally was completed. He had fought a good fight, he had finished the course, and he had kept the faith. He could die clear of the conscience of others. Can we say such in our time? Are we investing in such a way? Do we think Paul had some unique call that we can escape?

10

Paul to Others

The title of the class alone gives it special meaning. Having a "mission" speaks right to the heart of a man. I remember when I first heard about the class; it resonated so clearly, "As a Christian man, what am I supposed to do?" The Men with a Mission class helped direct me to not only "think" biblically, but also to "act" biblically. It was not just an exercise in how to properly interpret Scripture, though there was much that I learned about Scripture interpretation. The class answered so many burning questions in a forum that required me to study hard and use my heart, soul, and mind (Matt 22:37–40). The class connected me with other men who are on a similar journey, and together we made a three-year commitment to complete the class, the memory verses, and the homework. At times it was difficult, but it was always worthwhile. I now have the privilege as a graduate to work with the men on a regular basis, helping them establish biblical accountability partnerships. Second Timothy 2:2 has come full circle. Thank you, Pastor Wally.

—Personal testimony of Patrick Shurney
Columbia Bank Commercial Banking, Senior Vice President
Senior High Leader, Mount Airy Bible Church

Thank you for creating the Men with a Mission program. The past three years have been a tremendous time of spiritual growth for me. Your dedication to developing faithful men through this program has resulted in a very strong church leadership team of Men with a Mission graduates.

Men with a Mission has taught me the importance of quiet times, regular Bible study, and leading my family on a journey of continuous spiritual growth. During the three years of the program, I memorized more Scripture than in the last two decades, tripled the size of my Bible study library, developed friendships that will last a lifetime, and gained an accountability partner. My faith has grown, along with my desire to contribute to the growth of others. Thank you for investing your time, giving your energy, and demonstrating your concern for us!

—Personal testimony of Matt Schroeder
Senior Product Engineer, Fusion UV Systems, Inc.

PAUL TO EPAPHRAS

FIRST, WE WILL EXAMINE Epaphras. There are only three references to him in the New Testament, but it seems that he had some role in the early church via the apostle Paul. In Colossians 1:7, Paul calls him a "faithful minister." Paul says the Colossians had learned from Epaphras, which meant he had been some type of teacher to them. He also is called a "dear fellow servant." But then Paul adds in verse 8 that Epaphras declared unto Paul their love in the Spirit. It seems that Paul must have sent Epaphras there, or was just part of the process whereby Epaphras reported to Paul. It seems to be the same disciple-making process that we have been discussing—Paul to Epaphras, Epaphras to the Colossians. Colossians 4:12 adds further credence to this claim as Paul mentions that Epaphras labored fervently for them, that they would stand perfect and complete; they would be mature. This is the goal of the disciple-making process: maturity in Christ. Philemon 23 also mentions Epaphras as one who is with Paul in prison. Again, I can only imagine the investment at this time to Epaphras's maturity. Being in prison with Paul was surely going to be an adventure in the process of becoming more like Jesus.

PAUL TO EPAPHRODITUS

Epaphroditus is another one who Paul mentions in several passages. It is mentioned in Philippians 4:18 that Epaphroditus brought a report to Paul from Philippi. Maybe he also took the letter to them. We cannot be sure. The information about him in chapter 2 is most appealing. He is mentioned in this chapter with a host of others who have sacrificed greatly for the overall call of the gospel. Christ is mentioned first as one who gave His life for this goal. Paul then adds himself as one who was "offered upon the sacrifice and service" of his faith. Then he includes Timothy, as we have already studied, as one who will "naturally care for your state." Finally, he includes Epaphroditus. What an example this man is to all of us.

To get the best picture of this man's commitment to them, we must study the entire passage.

> Yet I supposed it necessary to send to you Epaphroditus, my brother, and companion in labour, and fellowsoldier, but your messenger, and he that ministered to my wants. For he longed after you all, and was full of heaviness, because that ye had heard that he had been sick. For indeed he was sick nigh unto death: but God had mercy on him; and not on him only, but on me also, lest I should have sorrow upon sorrow. I sent him therefore the more carefully, that, when ye see him again, ye may rejoice, and that I may be the less sorrowful. Receive him therefore in the Lord with all gladness; and hold such in reputation: Because for the work of Christ he was nigh unto death, not regarding his life, to supply your lack of service toward me (Phil 2:25–30).

There is so much about this man in this passage. This is really the only passage that helps us know anything about him, but what we learn is immense. Look at what Paul says about him:

1. He is my brother and companion in labor.

2. He is my fellow soldier.

3. He is their messenger—which may imply that he did go back and forth to Paul from Philippi.

4. He is the one who ministered to Paul—and I would imagine this involves taking care of the Philippian church.

5. He longed after them.

6. He was full of heaviness for them.

7. He had been sick—giving of himself to them.

8. He was near unto death for them.

9. Paul sent him eagerly.

10. He was near death, not regarding his life, to supply their lack of service to Paul.

It seems that Epaphroditus spent his life investing into the Philippians, doing all he could to ensure their growth. This is disciple-making at its ultimate sacrifice. Giving to others is costly, as we have already examined.

Ultimately, the investment of others could cost one his or her life. But should we expect it to be an easy life and an easy road? Did not our Savior, who modeled this, ultimately give His life? Did He not call us to give our lives to Him, not regarding our own life? Did He not call us to lose our life in His call? Disciple-making is costly, and Epaphroditus modeled this for us in a way to challenge us about our commitment to this calling.

PAUL TO APOLLOS

Another man who surfaces in the New Testament as one who was discipled and who discipled others is Apollos. He is first introduced to us in Acts 18:24. He is described as one who was mighty in the Scriptures. No explanation is given, but verse 25 says he was instructed in the way of the Lord. He had been instructed by someone, although the person is unnamed for us in this passage. But the clear understanding is that someone had invested into his life. What do we see Apollos doing? Verse 25 further adds, "He spake and taught diligently the things of the Lord." Apollos was practicing exactly what our Lord commanded. He was taking what he had been taught and was investing that teaching into others. This is exactly the heartbeat of 2 Timothy 2:2, but verse 25 also adds he only knew the baptism of John. Apparently whoever had discipled Apollos knew only so much to teach him. He was teaching to the fullest of what he had been taught. Verse 26 finds him teaching in the synagogue, the place of teaching.

As he was teaching in the synagogue, Aquila and Priscilla took him aside and "expounded unto him the way of God more perfectly" (Acts 18:26). He must not have known the fullest of the Scriptures, but he kept himself teachable. This is a key to continuing the disciple-making process. Never get to a place where you cannot learn more about what the word of God is communicating. Learning is a lifelong process.

Chapter 19 of Acts continues to explain Apollos's further stay at Corinth. He could easily have stayed there for a long while. It seems that after he was doctrinally taught, he used his time to continue to teach. By the time Paul writes 1 Corinthians, he already has a following (1:12, 3:4–6, 22). This following was placed on the scale of Paul, Peter, and Christ. Apollos's effort in the disciple-making process cannot be overlooked. Paul mentions in 16:12 that he was desirous to send Apollos to them. Paul apparently knew that Apollos could impact this church. Also, Apollos seems to be somewhat under the leadership of Paul, because Paul mentions that he could send him to them. Paul was clearly mentoring him in some way. Even in Titus 3:13, Paul is still exercising some authority over Apollos. He seems to be a disciple of Paul's who could be sent to help disciple others. Was this not the call of the early church? Is this not our call today?

PAUL TO TYCHICUS

Another important New Testament disciple is Tychicus. He is only mentioned a few times, but it is clear he also had a prominent role in the overall disciple-making process. Acts 20:4 mentions that he is traveling with Paul. Do we think that Paul just liked to have people around him? Do we think that Paul was fearful and needed a crowd? Was Paul ever unintentional about ministry? He is under Paul's leadership because Ephesians 6:21 says, "Ye also may know my affairs, and how I do, Tychicus, a beloved brother and faithful minister in the Lord, shall make known to you all things." Paul says he is sending Tychicus and that Tychicus is going to make known to them "all things." What are the "things" to which Paul is referring? Can it be Paul's health, his sick grandmother, or an ingrown toenail? This is doubtful. These "things" had to be in reference to the passion of Paul's heart—for all to come to the measure of maturity in Christ. It drove him and made his heart beat for the call of God. Paul was passionate about disciple-making, and everyone acquainted with him caught the vision. Is it possible our churches are not catching the vision because, as pastors, we are not living the vision?

Paul adds in Colossians 4:7, "All my state shall Tychicus declare unto you, who is a beloved brother and a faithful minister and fellowservant in the Lord." Paul was depending on Tychicus to invest in the lives of the Colossians, just as he did at Ephesus. He is included in the list at the end of 2 Timothy as one who was sent to Ephesus. Paul also says he is going to send Tychicus to Titus in Titus 3:12. Again, we see this man was under the leadership of Paul. How did Paul get this right or privilege? The real path seems to be that Paul invested in him, discipled him, and now was sending him out to do the same. It was Paul's passion. Is it ours?

PAUL TO OTHERS

We also could look at others, such as Zenas in Titus 3:13 or Erastus in Acts 19:22, who might be also mentioned in Romans 16:23 and 2 Timothy

4:20. Again, these are men who Paul seems to have some authority and right over. How did he get such a privilege? Although he was sent out as one of the first missionaries, there is no statement anywhere in Scripture where he was declared the overseer of the entire church. It appears as though he had the appointment because through his missionary endeavor of planting churches and disciple-making, he had personally invested into the lives of many who wanted to follow Paul. He even asked this of the Corinthians in 1 Corinthians 11:1, "Be ye followers of me, even as I also am of Christ." In other words, I am following Christ, so if you want to know how to get there, get behind me and let's go. It looks as if many faithful men agreed to do just this. Our belief in Christ is greatly connected to Paul's faithfulness to this process and the choosing of faithful men who bought into this passion. I wonder, what the chances are of the next generation catching our passion for disciple-making? Jesus asked people to follow Him (Matt 4:19), and Paul asked people to follow him (1 Cor 11:1). Why shouldn't we?

SPECIAL INSERT ON THE DEATH OF THE APOSTLES

It is important to review the deaths of the apostles. Some of this might be tradition or inaccurate, but the overall consensus seems to be that the apostles all died rather violent deaths, as shown below, except John, who spent his final years in exile. If just a few of these are accurate, it clearly states these men were willing to pay the ultimate price to see that the gospel went forth unto the next generation. This communicates disciple-making at its best—being willing to pay whatever price to see that it gets accomplished. I doubt any of us will have to pay for our calling the way the disciples did. But are we even willing to sacrifice a little?

1. John—martyred on the isle of Patmos

2. Thomas—preached in India and suffered martyrdom by a spear while there

3. Andrew—it is supposed he was crucified on a cross shaped like an X; hence, St. Andrew's cross

4. Simon, surnamed Zelotes—it is believed he died by crucifixion at an old age

5. James—was the first of the apostles to suffer martyrdom, having

been ordered to be beheaded by Herod in Acts 12:2

6. Peter—he was crucified head downward, feeling unworthy to die as his Master

7. Bartholomew—his martyrdom took place when pagans removed his skin and cut off his head with a scimitar

8. Philip—was scourged, imprisoned, and finally martyred by the spear

9. Matthew—died as a martyr, slain with a halberd

10. James, the less—his martyrdom came in Jerusalem when he was thrown from the peak of the temple, stoned, and his body cut through by saws

11. Thaddeus—clubbed to death by pagans

12. Matthias—served as a missionary in Judaea, where he was stoned and beheaded

13. Paul (an apostle out of due time)—suffered martyrdom in Rome[1]

We are not definite whether all these apostles died in this manner. However, the overwhelming evidence does suggest however that many, if not all, of these men lost their lives for the call of God. They were willing to go to any extreme to finish the call of God on their lives, and they were willing to pay any price. They knew the message must go forth, and they did their task well. Do we sense the same passion and call upon our lives? I believe every Christian is called to be a disciple-maker and must be willing to pay whatever price required by our Savior to see the task to the end. Regardless of what others may or may not do, may we sense the call and go forth for His glory? We do not have the option to any longer ignore the command of our Lord in the Great Commission. I pray it would not cost us our lives, but this should not stop us from obedience. The Great Commission is our call, and we must accept it as the early apostles did and invest wisely.

1. Lockyer, 247–60.

I Have Decided to Follow Jesus[2]

Chorus:

I have decided to follow Jesus.
I have decided to follow Jesus.
I have decided to follow Jesus.
I can't turn back, I can't turn back.
With the cross before me and the world behind me.
With the cross before me and the world behind me.
With the cross before me and the world behind me.
I can't turn back, I can't turn back.

Chorus

Though none go with me, still I will follow.
Though none go with me, still I will follow.
Though none go with me, still I will follow.
I can't turn back, I can't turn back.

Chorus

2. Thomas, 376.

11

Authorities on Disciple-Making

I am sure, given enough time, I could easily fill a book myself with all of the things that would be considered "changed in my life" since the beginning and completion of the Men with a Mission study, but maybe the publishers would opt for a *Readers Digest* version, so . . .

I can explain the impact Men with a Mission has had on my life with this very simple acrostic:

D   Demonstrate Christ living within me by the way I live my life—publicly and privately.

I   Invest myself in my wife, children, brothers, community, and work in a way that glorifies God.

S   Submit to His will, His work, and His calling for me, to remain teachable.

C   Commit to setting aside quality time for God through prayer, the study of His word, and ministry.

E   Encourage others to devote the time and effort to not only begin the Men with a Mission study, but to finish well.

R   Refrain from those things that distract my focus on Him, dilute my testimony, demean my brothers and sisters, or dishonor God.

N   Notice the opportunities God provides every day to reach, teach, win, and disciple others.

—Personal testimony of Brent Rutley,
Capital LLC, President and Founder
Head of Children's Sunday School, Mount Airy Bible Church

MANY OTHERS HAVE GONE on before me in the disciple-making process and addressed this essential component of the church. I hope the credibility of these men adds credence to the plethora of material already found in the Scriptures. Although some might conclude that I am belaboring the points in Scripture beyond the normal interpretation, others have come to the same conclusions.

LYN ANDERSON ON DISCIPLE-MAKING

One noteworthy work is by Lyn Anderson, *They Smell like Sheep*. He wrote an entire chapter on mentoring, which he said to be one of the roles God has given to the shepherds. He confirms this by pleading with the reader to "attract followers to them."[1] This is a key role of the mentor—a disciple-making pastor.

JOHN MACARTHUR ON DISCIPLE-MAKING

I am not sure if John MacArthur coined the term "Shepherdology," but he has a book with that title. It is a great title. It truly communicates much to the reader. I include this entire quote in the study to appreciate the breadth of these two important paragraphs.

> Discipling is a function that everyone must be involved in. It isn't optional. We're all to bring people to the knowledge of the Savior and go through the process of helping them mature. We're all to disciple whomever the Lord brings across our path. You will probably have different kinds of relationships with the people you disciple, but discipleship is nothing more than building a true friendship with a spiritual basis. It's not being friends with someone because you both like baseball, the same music, the same hobbies, or work at the same place. At the core of your friendship is an openness about spiritual issues. That's what carries a discipling relationship along.
>
> When you disciple someone, you're basically teaching him to live a godly lifestyle. You're teaching him biblical responses. A person is spiritually mature when his involuntary responses are godly. That's how to know if the Spirit of God has control in someone's life. In discipleship, you're to bring a person to the point where he

---

1. Anderson, Lyn, *They Smell like Sheep*, 74.

doesn't have to figure out how to act right, but where he can react right spontaneously.[2]

I am not sure I can add anything to what MacArthur says. He really sums up all that I have been trying to convey in this book. His opening quote is worth it all: "Discipling is a function that everyone must be involved in." In other words, there is no excuse for not disciple-making. It is our calling.

JAY ADAMS ON DISCIPLE-MAKING

See what Jay Adams said in his book, *Shepherding God's Flock*. He said, "Men who qualify for the work of the ministry are men who can keep the gospel torch burning brightly, so that they are able to pass it on (undimmed) to those who follow."[3] He said this in reference to 2 Timothy 2:2. Adams saw the importance of keeping the light burning. He saw that passing the faith along means more than sheer evangelism. It means investment, so they in turn can invest in others. It is an entire process.

WALTER A. HENRICHSEN ON DISCIPLE-MAKING

I like what Walter A. Henrichsen said in his book *Disciples Are Made, Not Born*. He said, "Making disciples begins with the task of evangelism. If we work only with Christians in our disciple-making ministry, then the net gain to the Kingdom of God is zero. Aggressive evangelism is the mark of the committed disciple, and it is primarily from the fruit of this evangelism that he chooses his Timothy—the person he seeks to disciple."[4] So, this is a process any of us can do and be involved with. There are billions of lost people all around us. Just find one, lead him or her to our lovely Savior, and go to work. Disciple-making will change both the disciple-maker and the disciple. I also really appreciated what he added to this study on page 100:

> Several years ago I was helping a young man who was extremely
> reluctant to witness. He was involved in beginning a student min-
> istry, so I asked him, "Joe, how many students on campus do you

---

2. MacArthur, *Shepherdology*, 50.

3. Adams, *Shepherding God's Flock*, 16.

4. Henrichsen, *Disciples Are Made, Not Born*, 77.

know personally? By that I mean, when they see you, they know you by name."

After having been there for a couple of months, he knew only two or three men. I said, "Joe, in the next four weeks, I want you to get to know as many students on campus as you can. Let's set our goal at 50 students. You don't have to witness to them. You don't even have to tell them you are a Christian. All you have to do is get to know them. Stop by their rooms and chat with them. Play ping-pong with them. Go to athletic events with them. Go to meals together. Do anything you want, but get to know 50 men so that one month from today, when I return, you can introduce me to each one of them by name."

One month later I returned to visit Joe on the campus and found that he had led six men to Christ. We didn't talk about whether he had gotten to know 50 people. We didn't have to. He had discovered for himself that as he became friends with "the publicans and sinners," the Lord naturally provided opportunities for him to share his faith. Witnessing, then, begins by establishing friendships with non-Christians.[5]

ROBERT COLEMAN ON DISCIPLE-MAKING

In the book entitled, *The Master Plan of Discipleship*, Robert Coleman puts an interesting spin on the disciple-making process.

> Considering that the church prior to Pentecost numbered only a few hundred believers, this is an astounding achievement. Probably the Christian community within three decades had multiplied four hundredfold, which represents an annual increase of 22 percent for more than a generation, and the rate of growth continued remarkably high for 300 years. By the beginning of the fourth century, when Constantine was converted to Christianity, the number of disciples may have reached 10 or 12 million, or roughly a tenth of the total population of the Roman Empire.[6]

He strongly suggests that the key to winning our world to Christ is not evangelism but disciple-making. As each new convert is matured, he is sent out like a mighty soldier after the training of boot camp. We do not send our soldiers into the battle until they have been properly prepared. We don't just let them enlist and send them. We don't drag warm bodies

5. Ibid., 100.

6. Coleman, *The Master Plan of Discipleship*, 39–40.

off the street and then give them a gun. We put them through a vigorous time of training so they will be prepared for the battle. There is grave concern that unless they are prepared, they might end up AWOL. Maybe this is why so many professing believers end up AWOL. They have never been through the spiritual boot camp.

WIN AND CHARLES ARN ON DISCIPLE-MAKING

Win Arn and Charles Arn together wrote a book titled, *The Master's Plan for Making Disciples*. This excellent work can best be explained by looking at how they define a disciple and then by looking at what they say is a true disciple. They say the Lord's mandate to His church was clear—to make disciples. They go on to give a six-fold description of a disciple. They say a disciple is a believer, follower, learner, witness, is baptized, and is a re-producer. Notice the clear disciple-making process. The disciple commits to follow, is trained, and only then does he reproduce this entire process into another believer who has chosen to follow.

I believe with all my heart that we have lost this passion in the church today. We can argue the issues of music, translations, the role of women in the church, spiritual gifts, different theologies, and a host of other important and necessary issues; however, the central problem with the church today is that we have either lost sight of Jesus's last command or reinvented it. We totally ignore it or say that it has to do with evangelism. Evangelism is definitely part of the process, but disciple-making is more than just evangelism. We have many in the church today who have professed faith, walked an aisle, raised a hand, signed a card, etc., but we have a depth of maturity that is alarmingly low. Christian marriages last the same as those without Christ. Christians are not better on the job either. They steal, cheat, lie, swear, and live as if they have not been bought with a price. The reason is possibly two fold. First, some are only professing faith and not possessing it. For the rest, they have never been discipled. There is much work to be done, and the fact that you are still reading this book is a sign that you might be one who is willing to do more than just talk about it.

LEROY EIMS ON DISCIPLE-MAKING

Listen to the foreword to Leroy Eims' book entitled *The Lost Art of Disciple-Making*. In this foreword, written by Robert E. Coleman, there are clear statements of the fact that the call of disciple-making has been lost. Eims goes on and further develops the same theme. Here are Coleman's words:

> Jesus came to save the world, and to that end He died, but on His way to the cross He concentrated His life on making a few disciples. These men were taught to do the same, until through the process of reproduction, the gospel of the Kingdom would reach to the ends of the earth.
>
> The way God's Son lived thus became a pattern to all who follow in His steps—a principle explicated clearly in the command to "make disciples of all nations." How they are made, of course, will be conditioned on particular gifts and roles in society, but everyone who believes on Christ is called to His work within his own vocation and life-style.
>
> Unfortunately, few Christians seem to understand what this means, at least when it comes to daily living. Even persons who are in leadership positions of the church often have no idea how to go about teaching others to observe all things that Jesus commanded. Where this pertains it is not surprising that believers fail to go very far in their pilgrimage of faith, much less develop the potential of their ministry.
>
> That is why this volume is such a pleasure to commend. It comes to grips with the real work of discipling men, not in vague institutional programs, but in clear guidelines for personal initiative. The treatment is simple and to the point. Our Lord's mandate need not be a lost art to those who will take to heart the counsel found in these pages.
>
> Giving authenticity to the book, while enhancing its down-to-earth appeal, is the author's own experience. LeRoy Eims writes as a practitioner, not a theoretician. For years he has been actively involved in shaping the lives of men. There are scores of persons today in harvest fields around the world who bear witness to his faithful labors with them.
>
> His approach reflects the strategy of The Navigators where he serves as International Ministry Representative. But what he says is not the property of any organization. This is basic New Testament discipleship. Anyone can profit from its reading. Best of all, the application of its truth can bring new meaning and excitement into living—living in the fulfillment of the great commission.[7]

There seems to be a consistent attitude regarding the importance of disciple-making. Many see that it was Jesus's agenda, Paul's agenda, and

---

7. Eims, *The Lost Art of Disciple-Making*, 9–10.

the early church's agenda. Many see it as a need that must be evaluated closely for the church. Yet many seem to never get past the realization of the need. Why, if we have the same Bible, are we so far diverse in how to communicate this important message? Maybe Satan has blinded our eyes to the overall importance?

12

Expect Opposition

When I started the Men with a Mission class, I had already been a Christian for more than twenty years and had read through the Bible at least a dozen times. I thought I had a good understanding of the Scriptures but had never attended a class like Men with a Mission. I thought I knew everything I needed to about God's word. Men with a Mission showed me that there was so much more I could be doing to mature my understanding of the Scriptures. Before this class, I had never really used a study Bible or any study tools, for that matter. I was mostly just reading the word. I wasn't really studying. Now I use a study Bible and make it a habit to look at more than the text I'm reading. I look at cross-references and commentaries. I also use Internet tools to cross reference other translations to get a broader meaning to the text I'm reading.

Men with a Mission also challenged me to consider ways in which I had not been applying scriptural principles to my life. I had never really been in an accountability relationship with another Christian before. Now I meet regularly with an accountability partner, and we review three or four areas of our walk with the Lord and pray for each other in areas where we struggle.

—Personal testimony of Phil Wasula
SRA International at NIH, Senior Network Engineer

"Trust in the LORD with all your heart, and lean not on your own understanding; in all your ways acknowledge Him, and He shall direct your paths." Never have these verses in Proverbs been more evident than after graduating from Men with a Mission under the leadership of Pastor Wally Webster. In this class, I was stretched further than I could have ever imagined. Memorizing Scripture was difficult for me, but God allowed me to remember many verses as part of our class work.

I help facilitate a small marriage group with my wife and four other couples. I feel Men with a Mission has given me more confidence speaking to groups of people. I'm not totally at ease with this yet, but the class helped me to get out of my comfort zone. When I lean on God, he makes all things possible. Thank you, Pastor Wally, for loving the Lord and being obedient to His word.

—Personal testimony of Jerome Bujanowski
Bowen and Kron Ent. Inc., Heavy Equipment Operator
Deacon, Mount Airy Bible Church

MENTOR CHURCH DISCIPLES

IT IS PROBABLY ADVISABLE to at least note some of the problems that are going to arise as we set out on this endeavor. We know the end of the entire process and rejoice for the two thousand-plus years of the fruit from the many who invested into disciple-making. We know it works, and we know it has the blessing of God upon it. This does not mean, however, that we will not experience hardship along the way. Just as God has promised to bless it, Satan will do all he can to destroy it.

OUR LORD FACED OPPOSITION

Take, for example, the life of our Lord. Scripture does not go into all the details about the life of Judas and the disruption he caused by being a nonbeliever in the midst of the work for God, and we can only imagine. In the process of disciple-making, we may find ourselves attempting to invest in someone who is not going to finish well. It usually does not take us long to realize this, and there is always the possibility that we might be wrong to judge prematurely. It is a hard area to understand.

Jesus had a privilege that we do not have; He knew the hearts of men. He was able to look at the past, present, and future and have an edge on whom He chose and the best path for each of them. Although we do not have this privilege personally, He promised in Matthew 28 to be with us always. We can be assured of His presence as we endeavor in this process. Nevertheless, it will be hard.

PAUL FACED OPPOSITION WITH JOHN MARK

I think of the many disappointments Paul had in the disciple-making path. He had to deal with John Mark in Acts 15. Apparently John Mark had left them earlier in Pamphylia (Acts 15:38), and Paul had to disagree with Barnabas about taking him. It caused much discontent, and therefore Paul chose Silas and went on without Barnabas. Barnabas chose John Mark, and they also set out. I do not believe this was best, because we do not hear of the work of Barnabas and John Mark together after this. I am sure Paul agonized many hours over this breakup.

PAUL FACED OPPOSITION THROUGH HARDSHIPS

In numerous passages, Paul warned of those who caused hardship in his ministry. Romans 16:17 says, "Now I beseech you, brethren, mark them which cause divisions and offences contrary to the doctrine which ye have learned; and avoid them." This is not the only place that he says this.

> Now we command you, brethren, in the name of our Lord Jesus Christ, that ye withdraw yourselves from every brother that walketh disorderly, and not after the tradition which he received of us. For yourselves know how ye ought to follow us: for we behaved not ourselves disorderly among you; Neither did we eat any man's bread for nought; but wrought with labour and travail night and day, that we might not be chargeable to any of you: Not because we have not power, but to make ourselves an ensample unto you to follow us. For even when we were with you, this we commanded you, that if any would not work, neither should he eat. For we hear that there are some which walk among you disorderly, working not at all, but are busybodies. Now them that are such we command and exhort by our Lord Jesus Christ, that with quietness they work, and eat their own bread. But ye, brethren, be not weary in well doing. And if any man obey not our word by this epistle, note that man, and have no company with him, that he may be ashamed. Yet count him not as an enemy, but admonish him as a brother (2 Thess 3:6–15).

In 2 Timothy 4:10, 14, Paul says, "For Demas hath forsaken me; having loved this present world, and is departed unto Thessalonica; Crescens to Galatia, Titus unto Dalmatia. . . . Alexander the coppersmith did me much evil: the Lord reward him according to his works." He also dealt with church discipline issues where a specific confrontation had to occur, such as in 1 Corinthians 5. In Galatians 2:9, Paul had to confront Peter personally about the details of the Law and its impact on believers whom they were discipling. It gets rather interesting because others in this process may choose to require different specifics for the ones that they are discipling. In the case with Paul and Peter, it was an issue of eating with Jews and Gentiles. Peter seemed to be playing both worlds. As we invest in others, there are sure to be examples where one direction or belief may conflict with another. Paul said in Philippians that as long as Christ was preached, he was going to rejoice. There is maybe room to disagree over preferences, but not absolutes.

I have seen this personally with the use of alcohol—the number-one drug in America today. Unfortunately, it is a legal drug. As much as there are some who like to argue that a little alcohol can be beneficial for one's health, I argue that the overall damage to our society and testimony outweighs any good that might come from a personal health advantage. One such brother of whom I am personally aware has chosen to defend his right to alcohol over the surrender of this right. It has cost him dearly already, yet he could have been a great champion for the cause of Christ. I have stressed greatly over the issue of cost. I cannot imagine giving something up for the cause is much of a sacrifice. Is this an absolute? Yes, in some cases; for this one brother, it is an absolute because it is keeping him from total surrender.

It is the same with the example Jesus used of the rich young ruler. God has used many wonderful, godly rich people for His work. As best as I can discern, He has never told them to give away all their riches. Riches are not in and of themselves evil. Yet, for the rich young ruler, they stood in the way of his progress. He had to give them up. He was not willing and went away (Matt 19:22). God is going to use the disciple maker to identify important issues and changes to the disciple required for the overall growth process. Because each disciple is different, the "rules" may vary. The point is that God is working to change all of us to be more like Jesus, and this path may be a little different for each of us. Some of us may be addicted to drugs, sports, television, politics, food, or whatever. Anything is capable of robbing God of the rightful place of ownership in our hearts. We need to carefully listen so we can discern what needs to be replaced, lest we leave sorrowfully as the rich young ruler. Are we willing to pay the price or suffer the loss?

PAUL FACED THOSE WHO LEFT THE MINISTRY

Paul alludes to the loneliness of this process in Colossians 4 after he has listed a number of men who have been with him in the ministry. Included in this list are Tychicus, Onesimus, Aristarchus, Mark, Barnabas, and Justus. Right after he mentions Justus, he says, "These only are my fellowworkers unto the kingdom of God, who have been a comfort unto me" (Col 4:11b). His point is that disciple-making is lonely. There were others listed, but these had a special place in this particular time of his ministry. This also is true of the work that is to be done today. There will be those who will only have seasons of influence in our lives. We need to redeem the time, buying up the fullest of these opportunities. They may be gone tomorrow.

In 2 Thessalonians, Paul warns once again about those who walk disorderly and not after the tradition, which was communicated from Paul (3:6). He continues, saying they do know how they ought to follow us. Paul was including other disciples who were finishing the course as those who need to be followed. He repeats this thought again in verse 9, "But to make ourselves an ensample unto you to follow us." He adds the importance of confronting a brother who is not living in obedience to the call. Remember Jesus said we are to teach them to obey (Matt 28), which I believe to be the foundation of the disciple-making process.

Early in his writing to Timothy, Paul warns about Hymenaeus and Alexander, who "put away concerning faith have made shipwreck" (1 Tim 1:19). Timothy was not to follow their example but instead, Paul's example of "war the good warfare" (1 Tim 1:18). Unfortunately for our disciples, there will be many casualties along the way, and they can become a deterrent toward finishing the goal. Paul had to continuously steer his disciples away from many bad examples. He often called them by name. Notice Paul concludes 2 Timothy with the story of Demas, which is probably the last book he wrote. If this is the same Demas as in Colossians 4:14 and Philemon 24, he at one time was faithful to Paul and the work of Christ. Colossians 4:14 says that Demas is greeting the Colossian churches. Philemon 24 says that Demas is Paul's fellow worker. In 2 Timothy 4:10, Paul says "Demas hath forsaken me; having loved this present world, and is departed unto Thessalonica."

Only someone who has invested hours into a brother can fully appreciate this pain. I look back over the years of many countless hours invested in those who later walked away just as Demas chose to do. Just the other night while out with my family for dinner, I saw a man who had been on a mission's trip with me and now no longer works by my side. In my early years of being a pastor, I tried to work with any man available. Hours were spent with some who later left the church because of some insignificant issue. One of the flaws of a men's discipleship ministry is that the wives sometimes do not see the big picture. If the wife is unhappy with something, she might drag her husband away because he would rather give in to her than lead by example. It will cost him in the long run, but it is better to see his weak leadership before he is in a leadership position.

In 2 Timothy, Paul also mentions Alexander the coppersmith. It is hard to know whether he is the same Alexander mentioned in Acts and earlier in 1 Timothy, but what we do learn about him from this text is enough to get Paul's point. Second Timothy 4:14 records for us, "Alexander the coppersmith did me much evil; the Lord reward him according to his works." The Scriptures do not record exactly what Alexander did, but Paul names him as one who did him much evil. We can only speculate, but for whatever reason, it seems this man sought to do Paul harm. Paul adds in verse 15 a caution to Timothy about Alexander by saying, "Of whom be thou ware also; for he hath greatly withstood our words." For Paul to doubt or accuse this man would imply a serious relationship. It is possible he was once a disciple of Paul's and unfortunately, he turned against Paul.

WELL-INTENTIONED DRAGONS

An interesting book was introduced to me when I first became a pastor. This book is part of a leadership series. This particular one is entitled, *Well-Intentioned Dragons*.[1] The title alone caused me to want to read it. There are many great insights in this little book, but the part that hit home most to me was about the folks who will reach out to the new pastor first. The author explains that the man who picks you up at the airport, the family who first takes you in, and the people who come the closest the earliest are the ones you are going to have the most trouble with. As a young pastor, I thought this rather extreme, until it proved to be true.

The family that was most instrumental in my coming to my first church housed us, fed us, and supported us early on and became a family that distanced themselves from us. Another family that catered to us early in our ministry soon became a true "thorn in our side." One family in

---

1. Shelley, *Well-Intentioned Dragons*.

particular was clearly becoming our best friends and for reasons I have never discovered, even after meeting with them, appeared to disrupt the ministry. Just recently I received a "death threat" from someone I invested many hours attempting to disciple. I am not sure why it has to be this way, but many pastors have shared the same stories with me. Yet, in spite of these failures, I have had the joy of many victories. It is like that last drive on the eighteenth hole or that long putt on the last green—it is reason enough to come out next week and try again.

Maybe this was true of Alexander. Maybe he was an early contact with Paul and became a real obstacle to him. There are several Alexanders mentioned in the New Testament, but this is the only one called the "coppersmith." Maybe this is to distinguish him from all the others. Regardless, Paul clearly says this man did him much evil. We need not believe we are going to have it any less difficult. Disciple-making is a difficult field of harvest. This might be another reason why some pastors ignore it altogether. It is like a song from years past; it is better to have never loved than to have loved and lost. I greatly disagree with this view. We are called to be disciple-makers, and we need not let the fear of failure rob us of going on with the process. We are going to have failures. These disciples are going to break our hearts, just as we far too often have done to our Savior, but the goal is worth it. "For what is our hope, or joy, or crown of rejoicing? Are not even ye in the presence of our Lord Jesus Christ at His coming?" (1 Thess 2:19). What a privilege to be part of this process!

INTERPERSONAL OBSTACLES

Another area that often is overlooked concerns relationships between the disciple-makers. We alluded to this earlier, and it is worth giving careful consideration to this issue. They say the number-one reason why a missionary might end up coming off the field is interpersonal relationships with their peers—not getting along well with other missionaries. The issue of pride, territorial control, and pre-eminence are serious. You would think we would understand and remember from the beginning we have been bought with a price and that we are not our own. Unfortunately, we far too often act as little children who just had a toy taken out of their hands. These disciples are ultimately the Lord's disciples, and we need to focus on doing all we can with the time allotted to us to answer this neglected call.

The Apostle John talks about this struggle with a man named Diotrephes. What a shame that all we know about this man is what is recorded for us in 3 John. Look carefully at these words in verses 9–10. "I wrote unto the church, but Diotrephes, who loveth to have the pre-eminence among them, receiveth us not. Wherefore, if I come, I will remember his deeds which he doeth, prating against us with malicious words; and not content there with, neither doth he himself receive the brethren, and forbiddeth them that would, and casteth them out of the church." This is such a sad commentary on this man. It looks as if he had his own agenda. Diotrephes missed the introduction to disciple-making, which clearly states this process is not about our kingdom, our agenda or our life. We were bought with the precious blood of Christ and given a calling that is irrevocable. We are on a mission that cannot be aborted. We cannot quit, retire, or change course. It has already been set.

> I'm part of the fellowship of the unashamed. I have the Holy Spirit's power. The die has been cast. I have stepped over the line. The decision has been made. I'm a disciple of his. I won't look back, let up, slow down, back away, or be still. My past is redeemed, my present makes sense, my future is secure. I'm finished and done with low living, sight walking, smooth knees, colorless dreams, tamed visions, worldly talking, cheap giving, and dwarfed goals.
>
> I no longer need preeminence, prosperity, position, promotions, plaudits, or popularity. I don't have to be right, first, tops, recognized, praised, regarded, or rewarded. I now live by faith, lean in his presence, walk by patience, am uplifted by prayer, and I labor with power.
>
> My face is set, my gait is fast, my goal is heaven, my road is narrow, my way rough, my companions are few, my guide reliable, my mission clear. I cannot be bought, compromised, detoured, lured away, turned back, deluded, or delayed. I will not flinch in the face of sacrifice, hesitate in the presence of the enemy, pander at the pool of popularity, or meander in the maze of mediocrity.
>
> I won't give up, shut up, let up, until I have stayed up, stored up, prayed up, paid up, preached up for the cause of Christ. I am a disciple of Jesus. I must go till He comes, give till I drop, preach till all know, and work till he stops me. And, when He comes for his own, he will have no problem recognizing me . . . my banner will be clear.
>
> —Written by a young pastor before his martyrdom in Zimbabwe for his faith. This article is public domain.[2]

2. Unknown, Leadership U, n.d.

This call is upon all of us, and there is no room for a Diotrephe attitude. Yet, we will discover that it exists in the disciple-making process.

Another biblical example of the same attitude can be found in 1 Corinthians chapter 1. Paul was writing to a much-divided church. He mentions in verse 10 that there were divisions among them, which he later identified as those picking who they were aligning themselves with. Some were saying they were of Apollos, some of Cephas, and some of Christ. Later in chapter 3, he returns to the same issue, "Who then is Paul, and who is Apollos, but ministers by whom ye believed, even as the Lord gave to every man? I have planted, Apollos watered; but God gave the increase. So then neither is he that planteth any thing, neither he that watereth; but God that giveth the increase. Now he that planteth and he that watereth are one; and every man shall receive his own reward according to his own labour" (1 Cor 3:5–8). Well said! There is no room for division on these issues. Our goal is clear—disciples are made, not born. Every Christian needs to be about bringing many sons to obedience so that the gospel of Christ can go forth. It is not about denominationalism, doctrinal preferences, or our agenda. The call is much higher.

We should expect opposition when it comes to the call of serving the Lord. He certainly dealt with his share of obstacles. He had to contend with the religious leaders, His own family, internal strife, and an insider sellout, not to mention the many times He was greatly misunderstood. Yet it seems to be the hardest when it comes from within our own camp. Believers spend too much time shooting each other because we believe God has given incredible discernment to us alone and not to the rest of the believing community.

Through the years, I have had countless brothers and sisters come to me and begin a sentence with this phrase, "Well, you know, Pastor, I have the gift of discernment." What this really means is he or she is getting ready to unload on you about something self-exalting. Oddly enough, I have yet to have one person come to me with the claim of discernment who has ever really had the gift. It might be discernment is one of those gifts that when you have it, you do not have to announce it. As Margaret Thatcher once said, "Being powerful is like being a lady. If you have to tell people you are, you aren't."[3] Likewise, if you have to announce you have the gift of discernment, you probably do not. This is a gift others

---

3. Maxwell, *Irrefutable Laws of Leadership*, 45.

recognize without you ever opening your mouth. And so it is in this area. Might we take a harder look at doing our best to disciple make instead of spending our time tearing others down for not doing it our way?

Our own experiences are not unlike Jesus's own disciples, who came to Him one day because there were some followers who were not doing it quite the way the "real disciples" were doing it. In Mark 9, our Lord rebukes the disciples over this mindset. His point is clear, "For he that is not against us is for us." Maybe we need to try to see the bigger picture about the call of God on our lives. If disciple-making is our goal, then let's do it for all we have, and leave the condemnation to others.

SATANIC OPPOSITION

Before we leave this topic, we need to address the attacks of the real enemy. Satan clearly does not want this process to develop in any church. I have seen his attacks from all directions first-hand. I have seen the pulls of other ministries, of well-intentioned dragons, of personal attacks, and a few not worth mentioning. Satan will do everything to destroy a focus on disciple-making. He knows if a disciple is truly made from the process, that disciple will be a force to reckon with for years. Plus, he knows once someone becomes a true disciple, the chance of producing more disciples continues to increase.

Obviously, Satan's first strategy is to get us to not witness. He already has the minds of the lost blinded, as he is the god of this world (2 Cor 4:4). Once he loses that battle and someone comes to faith in Christ, he then works diligently at doing everything he can to prevent that new believer from serious dedication to the cause. C.S. Lewis, in his classic *The Screwtape Letters,* explains the enemy's strategy of how Satan will do whatever he can to discourage the believer from the goal of maturity. Satan knows when he has lost a soul, but he has no intent of letting that believer become a true disciple. You can expect an all-out attack as you step out to begin the disciple-making process.

This is one reason why we see so many professed followers of Jesus Christ not living for Him. I traveled the same path for many years myself. This is why Scripture calls us sheep, and sheep need a shepherd. A shepherd does more than just feed his sheep on Sunday morning. A good shepherd makes sure his sheep are not led astray and grow strong to be fully matured sheep.

13

Shepherding

As I reflect upon my service for the Lord, I regretfully find many shortcomings. My involvement with church activities would lead one to think I was close to the Lord. My resume would read, "Deacon, Sunday school teacher, this and that committee." You could say I was plugged in but to the wrong outlet.

I found Jesus in 1987 at Elkridge Baptist Church, saved at twenty-seven years old. I was raised Catholic and had knowledge of God but not a relationship with Him. My Christian walk began to improve after studying Masterlife, a yearlong commitment focusing on John 15:5, being plugged in and bearing fruit. In 2001, this study took me out of my comfort zone to a motocross track to hold church for the unchurched. The ministry continues today; my wife and three children are involved also.

In 2003, our Baptist church had problems, and God led us to MABC. I learned how pride gets in the way of God's work. I thought I could teach this group about the Bible and quickly learned a lesson on humility. In humility, God teaches us that at our lowest point we are most useful.

I made a three-year commitment to Men with a Mission. I thought it was another class, another program. As I memorized 2 Timothy 2:15, I was led to devote more time to the study. My shortcomings became evident. I suffered from the pride of life; I needed a heart transformation. After three years of study, I am indebted to Pastor Wally. He selflessly gave so I could serve and teach with a different attitude. I am nothing. I know very little, but because of God's infinite grace and a humble heart, prayerfully, He can approve of my service. My resume now reads, "Training to be a humble servant." Paul said in Philippians 3:14, "I press toward the mark for the prize of the high calling of God in Christ Jesus."

Men with a Mission—more than a class or a program—is a surrender of your heart and mind to Christ Jesus. Press on!

—Personal testimony of Robert Lewis
Laurel KIA, Laurel, Maryland, Owner

BECAUSE WE INTRODUCED THE idea of the disciple-maker being a shepherd lightly in the last section, I want to spend considerable time developing this aspect of the theme. I have yet to see anyone call the disciple-maker a shepherd, but I believe this is precisely the idea. This very concept is substantiated throughout Scripture.

OLD TESTAMENT SHEPHERDS

The shepherd is present early in the Old Testament. Adam was responsible for the earth and its animals, and his children were taught to bring of the flocks to the offering of the Lord. Noah undoubtedly took sheep on the ark, and when Abraham was called to offer his son upon an altar, it was a ram caught in the thicket that came to the rescue. We continue to see the shepherd/lamb idea all through the history of Israel. Most of the Patriarchs were shepherds. God chose a shepherd to help His people out of Egypt. It was the lamb's blood that covered their sins so they could escape the Passover Death Angel. It was the sheep offering that permeated the sacrificial system. God called a shepherd boy named David as king to replace Saul, the failed ruler of man's choice. David was responsible for writing one of the most beloved Psalms, Psalm 23, which is again a picture of the shepherd/sheep. There are many more examples presented throughout the Old Testament.

NEW TESTAMENT SHEPHERDS

When we study the New Testament, this concept is still prevalent. Jesus is first called the "Lamb of God that takes away the sin of the world," and then He calls Himself the Shepherd (John 10). He is actually called the Shepherd in three perspectives throughout the New Testament:

1. He is called the Good Shepherd who gives His life for His sheep in John 10:11.

2. He is called the Great Shepherd who will enable us to become "perfect in every good work to do His will" in Hebrews 13:21. The word perfect here is the same word for perfect in Ephesians 4:12.

3. He is called the Chief Shepherd who is coming back for us in 1 Peter 5:4.

We see in this three-fold picture the entire plan of the disciple-making process. One first has to come to Christ in a salvation experience before he can begin the process. Both the disciple and the disciple-maker must be truly born again in order for this process to have any chance of actual growth. One cannot grow until one is legitimately planted in the true soil. Once this has happened, true growth is possible. This is where the Great Shepherd, the second picture, desires for all of us to travel. This is why He has called all of us to the disciple-making process—to ensure that all who follow will reach maturity.

God does not delight in those who backslide or who are lukewarm. Revelation 3:14–19 describes how He feels about those who profess Christ but are living a life that is not given to Christ. In our terms today, it makes Him "sick to His stomach." For example, the Laodicean city had a water problem. Someone came up with the clever idea to pipe water from hot springs and cold springs into the city, and therefore an expensive aqueduct system was put in place. The only problem was that by the time the hot or cold water arrived to the city, the water had become lukewarm and was good for nothing. In fact, when one tasted the water, one would spit it out. This is how our Lord describes a lukewarm Christian, and truly someone not involved in His Great Commission might qualify to be lukewarm. How would you describe yourself?

ENCOURAGEMENT AS A DISCIPLE-MAKER

Then there is the last picture of the Shepherd. Beautifully described in 1 Peter 5:4 is the finality of the process, "And when the chief Shepherd shall appear, ye shall receive a crown of glory that fadeth not away." This is quite an extraordinary encouragement about the end result that we can expect, and this verse does not stand alone regarding such encouragement. There are many more wonderful Scriptures that give us great hope about disciple-making. Philippians 1:6 is one of my favorites, "Being confident of this very thing, that he which hath begun a good work in you will perform it until the day of Jesus Christ." This is the day the Chief Shepherd returns to claim His flock. Our confidence in the disciple-making process comes from the great truth of the Great Shepherd. He is the Author and Finisher of our faith. He is the Alpha and Omega. He is the Beginning and the End, "Faithful is he that calleth you, who also will do it" (1 Thess 5:24). He has promised to be with us all the way to the end of the disciple-making process. He has promised victory. It is ours for the taking. Now choose five smooth stones, and go slay the giant!

So, we learn, the disciple-maker is, in a sense, a shepherd. As a guardian and caretaker of the disciple, a disciple-maker acts as the shepherd. This is why we see the heartfelt emotions of Paul throughout his writings. He talks about tears, pain, caring, and many other affectionate terms that resemble the care of a shepherd. Ultimately we realize the Lord is their Shepherd, and we minister as a shepherd under His authority. We lead them to the green pastures, still waters, and the correct paths. We walk with them through whatever they are facing. We eat with them, and we stay with them all the way through to the end. Once you embark on the shepherding/disciple-making process, it is a lifelong journey.

Jesus developed the same idea in John 10. Although once again we must be careful to remember that He is the Good Shepherd, we still work with His flock that He shed His precious blood for. He is the only Door, and we must point all disciples to Him and Him only. However, we still can be part of this process. It will be our responsibility to continue to hold their hands, help them hear His voice, help them to follow, help guard the door, stay with the sheep through the attacks, and be willing to lay down our lives for the cause. I realize we may never be called to lay our lives down, but this is the level of commitment necessary to bring a disciple on to maturity. The cause is worth it, but the laborers are few. Would you be willing to work in His harvest?

WE ARE OUR BROTHER'S KEEPER

Let's take this idea of the shepherd/disciple-maker one step further. There are thirty "one another" statements in the New Testament, and twenty-five are positive statements. I find trying to do all of these for the body of Christ at large to be quite difficult. By the way, these also are commands. It is basically impossible to do this well for the body of Christ, even in a small local church. Most believers feel defeated when they read the list and see how they fall short. But, what if the list was never intended to be for more than those whom the Lord has put in your life to personally disciple? The list then becomes reasonable and palatable. If all believers did their part to fulfill these "one another" commands to their disciples, every disciple/believer would be receiving exactly what Scripture has laid out for them. Here is the list:

(Positive Emphasis)

1. Mark 9:50 — Have peace one with another
2. John 13:14 — Wash one another's feet
3. John 13:34 — Love one another (John 13:35, 15:12, 17; Rom 13:8; 1 Thess 3:12, 4:9; 1 Pet 1:22; 1 John 3:11, 23, 4:7, 11, 12; 2 John 5)
4. Romans 12:5 — We are members one to another (Eph 4:25)
5. Romans 12:10 — Be kindly affectionate one to another
6. Romans 12:10 — In honor preferring one another
7. Romans 12:16 — Be of the same mind one to another (15:5)
8. Romans 14:19 — Pursue edification one to another
9. Romans 15:7 — Receive ye one another
10. Romans 15:14 — Admonish one another
11. Romans 16:16 — Salute one another (1 Cor 16:20; 2 Cor 13:12; 1 Pet 5:14)
12. 1 Corinthians 11:33 — Tarry ye for one another
13. 1 Corinthians 12:25 — Have the same care one for another
14. Galatians 5:13 — Through love serve one another
15. Galatians 6:2 — Bear ye one another's burdens
16. Ephesians 4:2 — Forbearing one another in love (Col 3:13)
17. Ephesians 4:32 — Be ye kind one to another
18. Ephesians 5:21 — Submit one to another
19. Philippians 2:3 — Esteeming one another better than themselves (1 Pet 5:5)
20. 1 Thessalonians 4:18 — Comfort one another
21. 1 Thessalonians 5:15 — Pursue good unto one another
22. Hebrews 10:24 — Consider one another to love and good works

23.	James 5:16	Confess your sins one to another
24.	James 5:16	Pray on behalf of one another
25.	1 Peter 4:9	Be hospitable one to another

(Negative Emphasis)

26.	Romans 14:13	Let us not judge one another
27.	1 Corinthians 7:5	Don't defraud one another
28.	Colossians 3:9	Lie not one to another
29.	James 4:11	Do not speak against one another
30.	James 5:9	Do not murmur against one another

There are several conclusions to be drawn from this list. First and foremost, it is virtually impossible for the church to accomplish on the large scale. The result is usually a defeated, frustrated attitude because the needs far outweigh anything one or two people can reasonably accomplish. Consider how many pastors must hurt internally because they are not meeting the needs of the flock. Yet, have we forgotten Ephesians 4? We are to be training our people to do the work of the ministry. What work is more important than disciple-making? What work of disciple-making should not include the "one anothers" found throughout the Scripture? Were they not modeled by Paul and others?

Second, the most important in this list based on sheer volume and well-established Scriptures is "love one another." What does this mean? How many of us really do this in the body of Christ? This phrase alone occurs fifteen times (John 13:34, twice; 13:35, 15:12, 15:17; Rom 13:8; 1 Thess 3:12, 4:9; 1 Pet 1:22; 1 John 3:11, 23, 4:7, 11, 12, and 2 John 5). The most any other one is listed is four times. All throughout the New Testament we are called to "love one another." Before someone comes along and accuses me of shirking this calling, I want to make it perfectly clear that I believe this is exactly what the text says. However, I also know for most of us, we believe we fall short in fulfilling this command. Just read one verse in 1 John 3:17, "But whoso hath this world's good, and seeth his brother hath need, and shutteth up his bowels of compassion from him, how dwelleth the love of God in him?" We have spiritualized this to include the need for prayer, but God just has not tugged at our hearts to do anything about this need. I am sorry, but this just does not work. Every true believer struggles when a fellow believer is hurting; when they are out of work, when they seem to have few clothes, when they have cars that break down, etc. Every true child of God wants to help, but we know this it is practically impossible. Yet a number of Scriptures seem to say the same thing. How can this be? I believe this is where the disciple-making process has fallen short. If I was personally assigned one family, one brother, or even a few, the task seems much more reasonable.

CONFRONTATION AS A DISCIPLE-MAKER

This also works in the area of confrontation. Many of us have had to go to a brother or sister and point out some area of concern. We believe that because we know the situation, we should to go to them. Has it ever occurred to you that maybe knowledge does not necessarily mean action? Maybe prayer is all we are to do; however, the one in the inner circle clearly has the edge. The mentor of the disciple has earned the respect and can fulfill Galatians 6 far better than someone from a distance. God is calling us to get closer to one another, but not necessarily closer to all. This is not even possible, so we mistakenly conclude that because it is not possible, we will do nothing, or whatever we can possibly do and deal with the guilt as it comes. The Lord's work, which often is immense, is often looked at this way and therefore, we end up doing nothing. Better to look more closely at the disciple-making process and realize that we can do a few things well, or a lot of things fair, and choose the best. Paul said that whatever we do, "Do it heartily as unto the Lord, and not unto men." Can any honest believers conclude they are doing the "one anothers" heartily if they are convinced it includes all, and they are only reaching a few? Most importantly, in the area of confrontation and accountability, one had better earn a close spot to the heart of the confrontee, or pain will truly follow.

Imagine the scene at the Last Supper, and you will be able to grasp this concept. All twelve were there, but it was much easier for Jesus to whisper into the ear of the one next to Him. This is why in Matthew 26:25 after Judas asks if he is the betrayer, Jesus answers, "Thou has said," and yet the disciples did not get it. Why? He was probably right next to Jesus. Jesus had his ear, although in this case it did not change Judas's response. Nevertheless, if we have the ear of our disciple, there is more of a chance that he or she might respond. One thing is certain for those of us who are presently involved in any type of confrontation; our present system is not working so well. Yet, to go to someone who has learned to trust us, the response has always been more positive.

Being a shepherd to one at a time, during a period of time, makes for a more realistic approach to the many demands upon the believer in the body of Christ. We know we are our "brother's keeper," but the needs continue to escalate beyond our reasonable ability. Why not train up the church to do the work of the church? Maybe the pairings by Jesus and the early church were more for this than we give credit. The needs within the church are continuing to grow, and the idea that the early church loved one another is what drew the community to our Savior. Today, the church is more about fighting and division. Maybe we need to take the church back to its own teachings, as commanded by Jesus to go into all the world and make disciples. How do you know when you have made a disciple? When they start reproducing after their kind!

REPRODUCTION AND DISCIPLE-MAKING

It is interesting that when God created the earth, He created the mission of reproduction. Bears produce bears. Fish produce fish. Birds produce birds. Mankind produces mankind. Christians produce Christians. We are not looking for more names on the roll; we are looking for champions who can change the world. At the rate we are going as a church, we are not going to see the changes we desire for our children. However, if in one year, each believer can lead one person to Christ and commit to disciple that person for three years, we could change this world for Christ. Maybe I am a dreamer, but I have an awesome God.

Most small-group ministries and care groups are attempting to do this, and some are doing an excellent job at reproducing themselves. However, some are more interested in the camaraderie than the call to reproduce. When you must break the group up to impact more for Christ, some do not want to do so. Have they forgotten why they are here? We have been bought with a price, and we need to glorify God with our lives. This world is not about us, and we need to get over ourselves. Disciple-making is about the Kingdom. Some small groups never mature beyond the "feel-good attitude," therefore, even after several years of investing in them, they are still just as needy as the day they began the small care group. If a care group or small group never gets beyond itself, it has missed the reason for its existence.

The same goes for the counseling department. Some folks are coun-seled only for the purpose of receiving help. This is a wrong approach. Some folks do need help, and they need to get help. But this is only one component to the process. Second Corinthians 1 clearly says we have been comforted so that we will be able to comfort others. This is part of why God pours anything at all into our lives—so that we may impact others. Disciple-making is designed to move us beyond ourselves into the lives of others.

14

The Goal

Men with a Mission has been a life-changing experience for me. Through this discipleship program, the Lord moved me from a place of complacency to one of deep desire to know Him more intimately. This class helped me mature spiritually and to understand and live out my role as spiritual leader in my home. I have become more disciplined in studying the word of God and have been able to apply these truths to my life as a Christian man, husband, father, and friend. My prayer life has become a priority, and my relationship with Christ has become deeper. My marriage is stronger. I have been challenged to study the word and not just read it for the sake of reading. I have been challenged to pay attention to being morally pure and to be accountable to men in the body of Christ. I now have the desire and confidence to disciple another man in our church and help other men become "men with a mission"—a mission to seek Jesus, know Him, grow with Him, and study His word that gives me life each day.

—Personal testimony of Marty Monroe
United States Postal Service, Letter Carrier/Supervisor

A T THIS POINT, WE should take a moment and clearly define our goal. Often we have trouble hitting a target because we don't know at what we are aiming. I heard about a man who once shot an arrow into the side of his barn and then went and painted the bull's eye around the arrow. Hitting the target may not be the best, especially if we are aiming at the wrong target. I believe many churches function this way. We may claim much success about what we are doing, but we may be using a false measuring system. So what are the marks of a disciple? What is a mature disciple? What is the target of the disciple-making ministry?

WHAT IS A DISCIPLE?

What is the definition of "disciple"? A disciple is someone who learns, adopts the philosophy and practices of the teacher, and lives the lifestyle of the teacher. A disciple can also be defined as a pupil or follower of a teacher or some school of learning. A more biblically focused definition would be that a disciple is a learner (Matt 11:25–30), a follower (Matt 3:14), and a reproducer (Matt 28:19–20).

The word disciple in the New Testament can be a verb or a noun. There are two verbs in the New Testament that are translated in the English as disciple. They are mathēteuō and manthanō. The first one only occurs four times in the New Testament (Matt 13:52, 27:57, 28:19; Acts 14:21). The other verb occurs twenty-five times. These verbs can mean instruct, teach, disciple, or learn. The idea is the disciple is one who is growing, maturing, and changing into the image of the one he is directed by. The noun is the more prevalent, occurring 268 times, most often found in Matthew and John with emphasis on the disciples of Jesus.

As you look closely at these terms, you will see an interesting connection between the word disciple and the word Christian in the King James Version. Matthew 28:19 uses the word for disciple, and it is translated in the NASB as "make disciple." The KJV says "to teach." But the heart of the word that Jesus wants is more than just teaching. He does not want us to just have information, but transformation. This is the difference between a disciple and one who has just been taught. If you study Acts 11:26, the early believers were called Christians. It may have actually been a mocking term, but it certainly has developed to be a cherished name. The text reads, "The disciples were called Christians first in Antioch." These disciples were behaving, acting, and looking so much like Jesus that they coined a term to describe them, "little Christ ones." This is the goal of disciple-making. We are not interested in just seeing lost people come to the saving knowledge of Christ. We greatly desire for folks to be saved; otherwise they will end up in a Christ-less eternity. We also desperately desire to see maturity. There will be some who will say it is not our job; it is the work of the Holy Spirit. I agree that maturity is the work of the Holy Spirit, but it is our responsibility to facilitate the process, or we would never have been called to be disciple-makers.

WHAT IS THE GOAL?

The goal is clear, "Till we all come in the unity of the faith, and of the knowledge of the Son of God, unto a perfect man, unto the measure of the stature of the fullness of Christ" (Eph 4:13). The goal is to become Christians, "little Christ ones." This is the goal of maturity—unto the measure of the stature (mature age) of Christ. If we believe this is going to just happen over time, then we need to take a closer look at the church today. Are we seeing this maturity as described in Ephesians 4 and other passages as the norm? Unfortunately, we are not.

Let's develop this picture even further. If we are going to describe a disciple, who ought to be the One given the opportunity to do so? Of course, the answer is Jesus. He coined the term, developed the plan, and modeled it for us. We need to have Jesus give to us the model to develop the disciple, and He does.

SEVEN CHARACTERISTICS OF A DISCIPLE

In Luke and John particularly, Jesus gives us seven characteristics that help make up the picture of what a disciple should be. This is the measure, the standard, and the goal that we need.

1. Luke 14:26: "If any man come to me, and hate not his father, and mother, and wife, and children, and brethren, and sisters, yea, and his own life also, he cannot be by disciple." Here our key word is disciple. Jesus gives a measurement to compare the individual disciple to a standard. What does this mean? It means a disciple is one who loves the Lord supremely, over any other relationship on earth, including himself. Our love is to be so obviously a love of deep devotion to Him that all other love relationships pale in comparison to Him. A disciple is one who is truly in love with Christ. Each disciple must be drawn to this love relationship above all others. From the words of Jesus: "If someone should be living a life where they do not love Him supremely, there is no way that they would be one of His disciples, because His disciples do love Him this way."

2. Luke 14:27: "And whosoever does not bear his cross, and come after me, cannot be my disciple." Again the wording of "cannot be my disciple" appears. Jesus is saying it is impossible for someone

to claim to be one of His followers and this not be true of them. This is the same as saying if anyone claims to be a true American, then they would recite the Pledge of Allegiance. It is impossible for someone to be an American and not be patriotic to America. This is His point. You cannot say you are a disciple and not bear His cross. What does this mean? If you saw someone in Jesus's day walking by you on the streets of Jerusalem carrying a cross, what would you think? You could easily say, "There goes a dead man." This is the cross-call for all of us. We have been called to die to self. We have been called to "lose our life so we can find it." This can only happen if we take up the cross, figuratively speaking, for full surrender to the Lord. We cannot be one of His disciples if we choose to live a life in the world and of the world, and claim to be one of His followers. This just is not possible, according to Jesus.

3. Luke 14:28: "For which of you, intending to build a tower, sitteth not down first, and counteth the cost, whether he have sufficient to finish it?" Jesus does not use the same wording as earlier, but this verse follows immediately after the first two that we examined. Notice the wording of "which of you," meaning "disciple." His point is that a follower must count the cost of what is expected of him on this journey to maturity. He is not saying that before you become a Christian to count the cost. A lost man cannot even imagine what the cost is to follow Christ. He is referencing this to followers of His. Listen followers: we are moving ahead with your disciple-making. Consider this: are you ready to pay the price of what it takes to be a true disciple? The following two verses mention that someone was not able to finish. The goal of maturity is to finish well. This also is the goal of disciple-making—finishing well. When someone comes to Christ for salvation, he or she cannot even imagine all that is involved in following Him. We just get out of the boat and begin walking. Jesus then brings us to a place where we have to decide whether we are going to be a true disciple. In John 6:60 when Jesus was preaching about the cost of following Him, some of His disciples had the response, "This is an hard saying." John 6:66 explains further their response, "From that time many of his disciples went back, and walked no more with him." They didn't count the cost. A true disciple counts the cost and is willing to pay the price.

4. Luke 14:33: "So likewise, whosoever he be of you that forsaketh not all that he hath, he cannot be my disciple." In the final verse of this passage, He reverts back to His original statement with which he began. "Surely if someone does not behave in this manner, they are clearly not one of My followers." This final verse is the culmination of all He has said. It comes down to full surrender and full consecration. Jesus is saying if there is someone who is not willing to give it all, he or she is not one of His. There was a story long ago told about a man who went to a revival service and came under the conviction of God. The preacher said at the end of the service if anyone wanted to be saved to come forward. The man leaned over to a man sitting next to him and asked, "Do we really have to go up there?" The man replied, "That's what the preacher said." But the man under conviction got up and went home. The next night he returned, sat in the same place near the same man, was under conviction about his sin again, the preacher asked the same question, and the man leaned over and asked the same to the guy next to him. The response was the same as the previous night, and the man went home frustrated. This happened again the third night, but with a different twist. When the man asked if he had to go forward, the gentlemen replied the same, but this time the man under conviction said that he was willing to go. Then the man next to him replied, "Then you don't have to go." You see, the question is not, are we willing to forsake all for Christ? I know of no one who has ever been asked to do so. But, more importantly, the question is, are we willing to say it is all His? This is where we must lead a disciple.

5. John 8:31: "Then said Jesus to those Jews which believed on him, If ye continue in my word, then are ye my disciples indeed." Here Jesus changed the wording a little, but the idea is the same. In this instance, the view is positive, whereas the earlier ones were negative. In this Scripture and the ones following are the proofs you are Jesus's disciple. The first one in this group covers the idea of perseverance. If you continue, which implies finishing well, this is proof you understand the issue of discipleship. The disciples in John 6 did not continue. First John 2:19 says, "They went out from us; but they were not of us; for if they had been of us, they

would no doubt have continued with us; but they went out, that they might be made manifest that they were not all of us." They did not continue. This is a strong part of the disciple-making process. It must be communicated there is not a place for AWOL disciples. Our calling is too intense and too important to shrink back. We are in the midst of war, and it is a battle that will be won—with or without us. The question then remains; whose side will you be on when it all is settled?

6. John 13:35: "By this shall all men know that ye are my disciples, if ye have love one to another." Again, in this passage, Jesus uses the more positive approach to disciple recognition. Our love one to another helps solidify the claim we are one of His disciples. You see, we love Him because He first loved us. We also love one another because the love of God has been shed abroad in our hearts. The early church disciples turned the world upside down, and a major reason was the way they loved one another. Acts 2:41–47 shows how attractive this faith was. No wonder many were added to the church! Would you not want to join with this crowd? Love is contagious, and we must direct disciples to the Lover of their soul. As we direct the disciple to continue to gaze into the word, we will be changed into the image of the Author. The Bible is the only book that makes us reflect the Author by studying it. The Author will make us more loving, as we discover just how much He loves us. A careful study of Scripture will help the disciple see that He is loved.

7. John 15:8: "Herein is my Father glorified, that ye bear much fruit; so shall ye be my disciples." One final time Jesus uses the wording, "So shall you be my disciples" as a reminder of the goal of the disciple. In this example, He is drawing the disciple to the call of reproduction, or reproducing after our kind. Just as everything that Jesus made in the original creation was created to reproduce and to reproduce after its kind, so it shall be with us who are a new creation in Christ. He expects us to go on to maturity and then become reproducers. We are supposed to take the things that we have learned from faithful men and invest in others so they too may become mature in Christ. This has been and will always be the goal of our Lord. He desires for all of us to be reproducers, but

we must be sure that we are worth reproducing. A disciple-maker will find that his disciple will want to be like him. We are then to be a man after God's own heart so what we present to our disciple about Christ is authentic Christianity. This is a lofty goal, and we need to remember whom we are serving.

These seven characteristics of a disciple help formulate the goal for the disciple-maker. We realize it is the Lord who produces this fruit in the life of the disciple, but this does not suggest we should not be intentional about what we are doing. Disciples are made, not born. Neither does being born again guarantee the process. Not all believers die as fully matured disciples. Some have chosen this present world as their ambition, and so will leave this earth with little or no maturity to show for a life with Christ. How sad. This is where we, as disciple-makers, must enter the picture. We must see that we are our brother's keeper and must do all we can to ensure they reach maturity in Christ.

I like what Paul said in 2 Corinthians 11:1–2, "Would to God ye could bear with me a little in my folly: and indeed bear with me. For I am jealous over you with godly jealousy: for I have espoused you to one husband, that I may present you as a chaste virgin to Christ." Notice his passion summed up with the word jealousy. I am passionate, Paul says, about your betrothal to Christ. This is the process, and we as believers are on this side. The wedding will occur later (Rev 19:7). Paul's desire, as ours should be, is to be more passionate about this process than anything else in life.

I often hear men say they just do not get excited too much about things, however, they will go to a football game and scream their heads off. They can watch their son play soccer and jump up and down. When it comes to passion for Christ, they cannot seem to find it. And the world passeth away, and the lusts thereof: but he who doeth the will of God abideth forever (1 John 2:17). We truly need a reality check on what is important eternally. And if we keep this before us, we will understand the only thing we are going to take to heaven, besides ourselves, are other believers. We are not going to take our houses, our yards, our trophies, our toys, our job, or whatever else that is going to burn. We are going to take souls. May we have this kind of godly jealousy, and may it burn in our hearts for the benefit of others and the glory of Christ.

15

The Biggest Obstacle

Men with a Mission (MWAM) helped me move from the sidelines to the frontlines. When I was first asked to join the Men with a Mission program, I said no because I felt I was still too young in my Christian walk. I felt that I didn't know enough to be around other Christian men who loved the Lord and were more spiritually mature than I was.

I had been a Christian for two years, but I was still on the sidelines. I was going to church on Sundays and prayer meeting on Wednesday nights when I could, but I was not reading God's word or regularly serving in a ministry. The next year when I was asked again to join Men with a Mission, I realized that nothing had changed in my life regarding God. I had not grown in my walk with the Lord, and I knew that a real relationship with Him was missing. I decided to trust that the Lord had put me in this church with Pastor Wally as my overseer, and if He thought I should go through the MWAM program, then I would give it a try.

I've heard many times that you will never regret growing closer to God, and I have no regrets. I am grateful for the opportunity that MWAM provided by challenging me to study His word, memorize Scripture, and discuss God's will and plan with other men devoted to learning more about God. God showed me clearly that His way is much better than my way. When He calls me to do something, I can step out and do it without fear because I am serving the One and Only who created me the way I am and loves me the way I am. The program helped me desire a deeper relationship with God, and every day He has shown me there is nothing that I should hold back from Him.

Since graduating from the program, the relationships in my life have become more centered on God—particularly in my marriage and friendships. My obedience to God's calling to serve others has also blossomed. When Pastor Wally asked me to serve in the Senior High Youth Ministry, I said yes, putting God's will ahead of my own. The Lord has shown me how to love others by building relationships with them and helping to encourage them to trust God and to follow the example that Christ set for us. I'm no longer standing on the sidelines watching others serve God. I'm with them on the frontlines for God's Kingdom, and I will carry the lessons I learned in MWAM with me throughout my life. I trust that by following God's will in my life, others will benefit.

—Personal testimony of Steve Hoyle
Orbital Sciences, Aerospace Engineer
Senior High Youth Leader, Mount Airy Bible Church

THE BIGGEST OBSTACLE WE all must battle as disciple-makers and disciples is the problem of "self." We live in a very self-focused world and society. Self-esteem has become the most important component of spiritual health today for the church. The next time you browse a Christian bookstore, notice all the self-help books written for the Christian community. In the dictionary, self is the most-hyphenated word in the English language: self-esteem, self-worth, self-appointed, self-taught, etc. We have no problem with the self-focus in our society. The problem is that the Bible teaches us to die to self. As a pastor, I can say it is the number one problem in the disciple-making process today. We have potential disciple-makers who are too self-absorbed to invest the time and potential disciples who are too self-focused to accept the call to maturity. We have a generation of believers who do not want to go to hell but have little interest in living the life exemplary of one going to heaven. The disciple-making process is the answer to such cavalier attitudes that invade the church. And what this process will do first and foremost, which is greatly needed in the church, is revisit the call of Christ for the believer to die to self.

G. D. WATSON ON DYING TO SELF

Following is an article by G. D. Watson. He was a Wesleyan Methodist minister and evangelist based in Los Angeles, California. His evangelistic campaigns took him to England, the West Indies, New Zealand, Australia, Japan, and Korea. He also wrote several books. He lived from 1845–1924. This might explain why he had such a good handle on this delicate issue. Here are his words:

If God has called you to be truly like Jesus in all your spirit, He will draw you to a life of crucifixion and humility. He will put upon you such demands of obedience that you will not be allowed to follow other Christians. In many ways, He seems to let other good people do things which He will not let you do.

Others who seem very religious and useful may push themselves, pull wires, and scheme to carry out their plans, but you cannot. If you attempt it, you will meet with such failure and rebuke from the Lord as to make you sorely penitent.

Others can brag about themselves, their work, their success, their writings, but the Holy Spirit will not allow you do any such thing. If you begin to do so, He will lead you into some deep mortification that will make you despise yourself and all your good works.

Others may be allowed to succeed in making great sums of money, or having a legacy left to them, or in having luxuries, but God may supply you only on a day-to-day basis, because He wants you to have something far better than gold, a helpless dependence on Him and His unseen treasury.

The Lord may let others be honored and put forward while keeping you hidden in obscurity because He wants you to produce some choice, fragrant fruit for His coming glory, which can only be produced in the shade.

God may let others be great, but keep you small. He will let others do a work for Him and get the credit, but He will make you work and toil without knowing how much you are doing. Then, to make your work still more precious, He will let others get the credit for the work which you have done; this to teach you the message of the Cross, humility, and something of the value of being cloaked with His nature. The Holy Spirit will put a strict watch on you, and with a jealous love rebuke you for careless words and feelings, or for wasting your time which other Christians never seem distressed over.

So make up your mind that God is an infinite Sovereign and has a right to do as He pleases with His own, and that He may not explain to you a thousand things which puzzle your reason in His dealings with you. God will take you at your word; if you absolutely sell yourself to be His slave, He will wrap you up in a jealous love and let other people do and say many things that you cannot. Settle it forever; you are to deal directly with the Holy Spirit, He is to have the privilege of tying your tongue or chaining your hand or closing your eyes in ways which others are note dealt with. However, know this great secret of the Kingdom: When you are so completely possessed with the living God that you are, in your secret heart, pleased and delighted over this peculiar, personal, private, jealous guardianship and management of the Holy Spirit over your life, you will have found the vestibule of heaven the high calling of God.[1]

AS TAUGHT BY OUR LORD

Dying to self was a clear principle taught by our Lord to His disciples. He realized if someone was to be His follower, he or she was going to have to accept in advance who was really in charge. God was going to take the disciple through hours of training, and if he or she was not willing to fight these battles, it was going to be a long and tiring battle for the disciple-maker. Jesus spoke many times on this subject. The following are a few examples:

1. Matthew 6:19–33: Especially note verse 33. "But seek ye first the kingdom of God, and his righteousness; and all these things shall be added unto you." The key is to put forth a concerted effort to live a life fully and completely toward Christ, not relish selfish ambition.

2. Matthew 8:18–22: Jesus addresses a certain scribe and another disciple who have come to Him to follow Him wherever He goes. He makes it clear that it will cost them greatly, and they must be willing to sacrifice, even to the point of comfort and family pulls.

3. Matthew 10:32–39: He makes it clear we are to "lose our life for His sake." What does this mean? Verse 39 says, "He that findeth his life shall lose it: and he that loseth his life for my sake shall find it." Losing one's life is synonymous with dying to self. In other words, we must be willing to forego our wishes and be fully surrendered to His call for our lives. Disciples will tell you it is a tough life to live, but not impossible, because Jesus has called us to do it.

4. Matthew 16:24–28: This verse is a further explanation of the passage in chapter 10. Look particularly at verses 24–26, "Then

1. Watson, *awildernessvoice.com.*

said Jesus unto his disciples, If any man will come after me, let him deny himself, and take up his cross, and follow me. For whosoever will save his life shall lose it; and whosoever will lose his life for my sake shall find it. For what is a man profited, if he shall gain the whole world, and lose his own soul? or what shall a man give in exchange for his soul?" I don't think there needs to be much commentary on these verses. Jesus is clearly calling His followers to die to self and follow Him. Men spend far too much time in this world trying to gain this world, which is passing away (1 John 2:15–17). We need to be called to the higher call.

5. Mark 10:17–22: Here we see the story of the rich young ruler. Jesus would not permit this man to follow him unless he gave up his riches. Why? Because Jesus knew his riches were a barrier to his maturity. Riches do not always cause someone to experience a lack of growth; however, Jesus knew it to be so for this man. He also knows our hindrance. He will call us to give up, surrender, and die to self. It is part of the journey.

6. Mark 10:35–45: This is an interesting story about two of Jesus's disciples who were vying for the lead role once He left this earth. Jesus concludes this section with an amazing few verses about the call of God on our lives. He said, "But so shall it not be among you; but whosoever will be great among you, shall be your minister; And whosoever of you will be the chiefest, shall be servant of all. For even the Son of man came not to be ministered unto, but to minister, and to give his life a ransom for many" (Mark 10:43–45). Jesus not only taught dying to self—He also lived it. Philippians 2:6–8 further explains this exact thought. "Who, being in the form of God, thought it not robbery to be equal with God; But made himself of no reputation, and took upon him the form of a servant, and was made in the likeness of men; And being found in fashion as a man, he humbled himself, and became obedient unto death, even the death of the cross." Jesus is not asking for something from His followers that He was not willing to do Himself. Go and do thou likewise.

7. Mark 14:36: This verse takes us into the Garden of Gethsemane. His words to the Father make it adequately clear He has no personal agenda. "Take away this cup from me; nevertheless not

what I will, but what thou wilt." In other words, whatever You desire for Me is what I am going to do. This is called dying to self, and unless a disciple can understand this, he or she is going to struggle with the call of God to maturity for him or her. This call cannot be served by a mere profession of faith. This is a call of complete sacrifice and service for the King.

8. Luke 14:25–33: We examined these verses earlier, and they are worthy of mentioning again. The call is to "forsake all." The last time I checked, that word "all" in the Greek actually meant "all." The call is severe and the cost is great, but the reward is out of this world.

9. John 13:1–17: Here we see the final scene in the life of our Lord prior to His crucifixion. He takes the disciples and washes their feet. I can only imagine when Peter and John prepared the room for the Passover, what must have gone through their minds. They would have had to put the bowl, the towel, and the basin near the door and then concluded they were never going to do this slave chore. A servant often washed the feet of guests as they came to the house. All of the rest of the disciples must have thought the same thing, for not one of them even made an effort to pick up the towel. In my wild way of looking at things, I bet it was put in such a way that you had to step over it or go around it. It was going to be a visual that our Lord would imbed in their minds forever. Notice how He closes this section. "Ye call me Master and Lord; and ye say well; for so I am. If I then, your Lord and Master, have washed your feet, ye also ought to wash one another's feet. For I have given you an example, that ye should do as I have done to you. Verily, verily, I say unto you, the servant is not greater than his lord; neither he that is sent greater than he that sent him. If ye know these things, happy are ye if ye do them" (John 13:13–17). Do you know what Jesus is teaching? He is teaching that He wants us to die to self in our service for Him. If it means washing the feet of others, so be it. We are called to do His bidding, not be about our world and our agenda. This is our Father's world, not ours.

JESUS'S FOLLOWERS UNDERSTOOD DYING TO SELF

Here are a few examples where our Lord taught this great theme. This is certainly not an exhaustive list, but it should be enough to point out how serious Jesus is about His call to His disciples to take up their cross (to die) and follow Him. This theme was obviously understood by the early church because many of them chose such a path of surrender and sacrifice to the cause. They also taught such to the followers as is evidenced by their writings.

1. Romans 12:1–2: Paul calls us to present ourselves a living sacrifice.

2. Romans 14:8: "For whether we live, we live unto the Lord; and whether we die, we die unto the Lord; whether we live therefore, or die, we are the Lord's."

3. 1 Corinthians 6:19–20: It is clear that we have been bought with a price, we are not our own, and therefore have no rights.

4. 2 Corinthians 4:7–18: It might be best to at least quote two verses from this passage. "Always bearing about in the body the dying of the Lord Jesus, that the life also of Jesus might be made manifest in our body. For we which live are always delivered unto death for Jesus' sake, that the life also of Jesus might be made manifest in our mortal flesh" (2 Cor 4:10–11). Clear verses, are they not?

5. Galatians 2:20: "I am crucified with Christ; nevertheless I live; yet not I, but Christ liveth in me; and the life which I now live in the flesh I live by the faith of the Son of God, who loved me, and gave himself for me."

6. Galatians 6:14: "But God forbid that I should glory, save in the cross of our Lord Jesus Christ, by whom the world is crucified unto me, and I unto the world."

7. Philippians 2:3: "Let nothing be done through strife or vainglory; but in lowliness of mind let each esteem other better than themselves."

8. Colossians 3:2–3: "Set your affection on things above, not on things on the earth. For ye are dead, and your life is hidden with Christ in God."

9. 2 Timothy 2:11: "It is a faithful saying; For if we be dead with him, we shall also live with him."

10. Titus 2:14: "Who gave himself for us, that he might redeem us from all iniquity, and purify unto himself a peculiar people, zealous of good works."

One need not think these are isolated verses. Scripture is clear we are not our own, we have been purchased by Jesus's precious blood, and we need to live our lives under His sovereign control. To be in the rightful place, we need to be obedient to the things He has taught us. Jesus said it well, "If you love me, keep my commandments." The commandments certainly include His last one, which He has given to all who follow Him: "Go out and make disciples." This again is not a call merely to evangelism, but to the maturity process. He has called us to be disciple makers. Now go and do it.

ONE MORE ARTICLE ON DYING TO SELF

Following is an article that I have in my notes but was unable to find the source. It is about dying to self. Please read this prayerfully.

> When you are forgotten or neglected or purposely set at naught, and you sting and hurt with the insult of the oversight, but your heart is happy, being counted worthy to suffer for Christ—that is dying to self. When your good is evil spoken of, when your wishes are crossed, your advice disregarded, your opinions ridiculed and you refuse to let anger rise in your heart, or even defend yourself, but take it all in patient loving silence—that is dying to self. When you lovingly and patiently bear any disorder, any irregularity, or any annoyance, when you can stand face to face with waste, folly, extravagance, spiritual insensibility, and endure it as Jesus endured it—that is dying to self. When you are content with any food, and offering, any raiment, any climate, any society, any attitude, any interruption by the will of God—that is dying to self. When you never care to refer to yourself in conversation, or to record your own good works, or itch after commendation, when you can truly love to be unknown—that is dying to self. When you see your brother prosper and have his needs met and can honestly rejoice with him in spirit and feel no envy nor question God, while your own needs are far greater and in desperate circumstances—that is dying to self. When you can receive correction and reproof from

one of less stature than yourself, can humbly submit inwardly as well as outwardly, finding no rebellion or resentment rising up within your heart—that is dying to self.

—*AUTHOR UNKNOWN*

16

Getting Started

I don't know if I can write a testimony of how Men with a Mission has impacted my life without starting at the beginning, since I believe it was a life-changing experience for me.

I surrendered my life to God through the faithful testimony of my wife, Pam, and the reading through God's word several times, but since there was no mentoring or instruction after my public profession, I was still clueless. I was brought up in a Christian Science church. The Bible was used, but the truth of Scripture is revealed, they believe, by Mary Baker Eddy in her *Key to the Scriptures.* I did not have a biblical understanding of Jesus Christ or any knowledge that the Bible is God's inerrant word.

Since there was no biblical training at the church I was attending, there was no growth on my part, but there was a desire to understand God through His word. The desire became overshadowed by life. I started a business, which took all my focus. Little did I know that God is always faithful in carrying out His plan for those who come to Him through trust and faith.

We bought property and built a house in Mount Airy. After the house was complete—is it ever?—Pam started attending churches in the area; I was concentrating all my efforts on the house. Pam narrowed the search down and wanted to start attending, but I wasn't interested. I had "been there done that." Even after selling the house for three times what we bought it for, finding fifteen acres for a third of what it should have sold for, and realizing one of my dreams of building my own home, I had not seen God's hand in all of this.

We started attending what was then Lisbon Bible Church and is now Mount Airy Bible Church. Through the conviction of the preaching of God's word, I had to know the God of the Bible. This time it was a burning desire, but since I knew little or nothing about the Scriptures, I didn't even know how to go about studying the Bible.

One day I got up enough courage to ask Pastor Wally if he would mind showing me how to study the Bible. He agreed, and we began meeting about twice a month. I had to endure the teasing of Pastor's wife, Vicky, who accused me of stealing her time with her husband. We began by going through prepared Bible studies, but they always left us feeling a little flat. The studies never really met my need, and after a while we just met and prayed together.

A year or so later, Pastor started a leadership training class, and I did not sign up because I never felt qualified to be a leader in the church. Two years later, he invited several men to attend the class, and this time I accepted. Through Pastor's teaching and patience, we began to learn the truth of God's word and how to apply it to our lives, over and over until God's truth was our lives.

Pastor Wally could have directed me to a Bible college or other courses of study, which I am sure I would have given up on, but since Pastor Wally invested his time, I was willing to invest mine. After two years of Leadership Training—I believe it was the same for both years—we began our third and last year, Eldership Training.

Now I thought I would never be qualified to be an elder and never had any intention of becoming an elder, but I took the class anyway because it was my desire to become a man of God. Through God's grace and faithfulness and Pastor Wally's faithfulness and teaching, I became a deacon and am now serving as an elder at Mount Airy Bible Church, and yes, I am still taking classes at a Bible college.

Currently I am trying to develop a high school curriculum that will grab our high school students the same way Pastor Wally's Men with a Mission grabbed me and changed it from a life of following along as James 1:6 states "like a wave of the sea driven with the wind and tossed" and train them as Colossians 2:8 states, "Beware lest any man spoil you through philosophy and vain deceit, after the tradition of men, after the rudiments of the world, and not after Christ."

To say that Men with a Mission had an impact on my life would be an understatement. and I give all honor and glory to God, as I know Pastor Wally would, for His faithfulness in producing fruit through His word, but it also took a faithful man who said, "Here am I, I will tend your sheep."

—Personal testimony of Maarten vanHemert
Elder, Mount Airy Bible Church

IF YOU HAVE READ this far, I know that the Holy Spirit has gripped your heart about Jesus's last commandment to make disciples. You may not be sure how to get started. I did not know until the Lord helped me see what His overall plan was. Because I do not like to reinvent the wheel, let me offer some practical suggestions for your journey.

First, my entire three-year discipleship program is available on CD, can be used as a PowerPoint presentation, or can simply be used the old-fashioned way of classroom teaching section-by-section. You could also adapt it by using both. The choice is yours.

Second, I am personally available to help in any way I can. I certainly do not consider myself to be the one with all the answers, but after doing this for over fifteen years intentionally and approximately thirty years overall in ministry, I believe God has given me some answers. Please go to our website www.mabcmd.org and contact us for more information or help. We so believe in this mission that we are making ourselves available to your needs.

Third, let me offer some step-by-step suggestions:

1. Prayer. I cannot stress enough how important this part of the process is for success. Not only should the disciple-maker be a man of prayer, but he also needs to develop the hunger for prayer in the heart of the disciple. Jesus was such a man of prayer that the disciples came to Him and asked Him to teach them to pray (Luke 11:1). There was nothing in this request about how to pray. They just said, "Teach us to pray. Not teach us how, but bring us to the place where prayer is as central in our lives as it is Yours." May this process be bathed in prayer, especially as you attempt to get it off the ground. Pray about who to contact, who to give this book to, who to disciple, and how to approach your board or pastors. This must be done with prayer.

2. Patience is the most operative word. Not everyone is ready for this process to be implemented, and we should be careful how we approach the process. Give the leadership time to bathe it in prayer. Give the leadership time to do their homework. Give the leadership time to sort out all the specifics. And please remember, this is His church, and He will build it as He sees fit. If your church never accepts this as part of their responsibility, you

can always personally be a disciple maker. God will honor your commitment to training up faithful men.

3. Practice. In other words, get your hands in the soil and go for it. We spend far too much time in the body of Christ talking about what needs to be done and not enough time doing what needs to be done. You can begin first by leading someone to Christ. There are billions of lost people waiting to hear the gospel. If we are faithful in sharing it, we will eventually find someone whose heart the Lord is preparing. We started lighting a candle every Sunday morning after someone comes to Christ via the ministry of the people of our church. The stories have been so heartwarming that the church has taken the passion of evangelism to a higher level. When we first began, I feared we would have many Sundays with no converts. However, to my lack of faith and shame, there is rarely a Sunday when someone does not come to Christ. We have many Sundays blessed with multiple people finding and accepting Christ. Some come through personal evangelism at work and some come through ministry in the church. Evangelism is contagious. If you have not led anyone to Christ, I challenge you to get out there and tell people about Jesus. There are folks just waiting to hear from you about Christ. If you already have someone who is a new or immature believer, you can start with him or her. Either way is certainly permissible, because our goal is seeing every believer as mature in Christ. You can and should tell them right up front that you desire to invest in their lives and disciple them. Very few new believers will ever turn you down. They are so on fire for the Lord; this is the ideal time to take them to the next level. Waiting too long allows them time to get around a bunch of stale older believers, and then it would be too late. Earlier is better.

4. Program. There is no perfect program that I am aware of, but I would like to suggest you take a look at the program that God has put together at our church. It is in a format that is readable and adaptable. You can use a booklet form and proceed question by question. If you desire a class setting with several disciples, it also is in a CD format you can use with PowerPoint and other similar newer technological advances.

Now that you have a disciple, here are some hints.

- Meet at least two times per month. You can do more, but anything less is too infrequent to make a difference.

- Memorize the Scriptures. Hiding God's word in their hearts is an absolute. I have never met a disciple yet who could not memorize.

- Be sure to do all the work. Each assignment helps build for a larger call.

- Commit to at least a one-year plan. I believe three years is better, but you might find that your disciple is not going to commit as needed. You might need to move on to someone else because he is not fulfilling his commitment.

Stay focused on this project. It may seem daunting at first, but give God time to do a work honoring to Him. You will be amazed at the results of this intensive study and commitment to God and His word. In one year, you and your disciple will have memorized more Scripture than you ever knew you could, wrestled with more issues than you have ever thought about, and seen the hand of God moving like never before. It works. Praise the Lord.

In closing, let me share a story that may summarize my heart:

I PLEDGE ALLEGIANCE

Captain John S. McCain, a retired U. S. Navy officer and a U. S. Senator from Arizona and ran against President George W. Bush for the Republican Party nominations during the 2000 Presidential Election, spent five and one-half years as a prisoner of war during the Vietnam War. During the early years of his imprisonment, the North Vietnamese Army kept him and his comrades in solitary confinement or with only two or three prisoners in a cell.

In 1971 McCain was moved out of isolation into a large room with thirty or forty other prisoners. Captain McCain says this was a wonderful change that came about because of the efforts of millions of Americans on behalf of the POWs.

One of the men moved into the room with McCain was named Mike Christian. Mike came from a small town near Selma,

Alabama, where he lived with his rather poor family. In fact, Mike didn't even wear shoes until he was about thirteen years old.

At age seventeen, Mike enlisted in the U. S. Navy. He later earned a commission by going to Officer Training School. Still later, he became a Naval Flight Officer and was assigned to the Vietnam conflict where he was eventually shot down and captured in 1967. Mike had a keen appreciation for the opportunities that America and her military provided for people who want to work and succeed.

As part of the improved treatment by the Vietnamese, some prisoners were allowed to receive packages from home. Some of these packages yielded small items of clothing, such as handkerchiefs and scarves. From these items, and using a bamboo needle that he found, Mike created an American flag, which he sewed onto the inside of his shirt.

Every afternoon, before they ate their standard bowl of soup, the American prisoners would hang Mike's shirt on the wall of the cell and, with their hands over their hearts; they would sincerely repeat the Pledge of Allegiance. The Pledge of Allegiance may not seem like the most important part of our day now, but in that stark, dank cell, it was indeed a most important and meaningful event.

One day the Vietnamese searched the Americans' cell, as they did periodically. They discovered Mike's shirt with Old Glory sewn inside and removed it. That evening they returned, opened the cell door, and beat Mike Christian severely for the next couple of hours in front of Captain McCain and the other prisoners. Then they threw him back inside the cell and locked the door.

"We cleaned Mike's wounds as best we could," said Captain McCain, "and helped him onto the concrete slab in the middle of the cell on which we slept."

Later, after the excitement had died down, McCain looked over to where they had laid Mike, but he was gone. Dusk had settled on the camp, so the cell was dark, and it was difficult to see. There were only four small, dim light bulbs in the large room, one in each corner.

Finally, Captain McCain's eyes found Mike. He had painfully braced himself up in the corner under one of the dim lights. His eyes were swollen almost shut from the beating they had given him, and blood was oozing from around the make-do bandages they had tied around his head and arms. There, with a piece of red cloth, another shirt, and his bamboo needle, Mike Christian was slowly making another American flag.

Captain McCain said the other prisoners asked each other, "Why? Why is he doing it? The Vietnamese will just find it too, sooner or later, and next time they might kill him." Mike wasn't making the flag because it made him feel better. He was making the flag because he knew how important it was to the other Americans to be able to pledge their allegiance to their flag and homeland. And, indeed, those Americans never took the Pledge of Allegiance for granted again.[1]

May we not take the Christ-call upon our lives for granted either!

1. Hollingsworth, *Fireside Stories of Love, Life, and Laughter*, 101–103.

Bibliography

Adams, Jay E. *Shepherding God's Flock*. Grand Rapids: Zondervan Publishing House, 1975.

Anderson, Leith. *Leadership That Works*. Minneapolis: Bethany House Publishers, 1999.

Anderson, Lynn. *They Smell Like Sheep*. West Monroe: Howard Publishing Company, 1997.

Anderson, Robert C. *The Effective Pastor*. Chicago: Moody Press, 1985.

Arn, Charles, and Win Arn. *The Master's Plan for Making Disciples*. Grand Rapids: Baker Books, 1998.

Barna, George. *Building Effective Lay Leadership Teams*. Ventura: Issachar Resources, 2001.

———. *Growing True Disciples*. Ventura: Issachar Resources, 2000.

Barrs, Jerram. *Shepherds & Sheep*. Downers Grove: InterVarsity Press, 1983.

Billig, Robert. *Les Miserables*. Comp. Claude-Michel and Kretzmer, Herbert Schönberg. 1986.

Blackaby, Henry T., and Richard Blackaby. *Spiritual Leadership*. Nashville: B&H Publishing, 2001.

Boice, James Montgomery. *Christ's Call to Discipleship*. Grand Rapids: Kregel Publications, 1986.

Bruce, A.B. *The Training of the Twelve*. Grand Rapids: Kregel Classics, 1971.

Clinton, Dr. J. Robert. *The Making of a Leader*. Colorado Springs: NavPress, 1988.

Coleman, Robert E. *The Master Plan of Discipleship*. Old Tappan: Fleming H. Revell Company, 1987.

Eims, Leroy. *Be the Leader You Were Meant to Be*. Wheaton: Victor Books, 1975.

———. *The Lost Art of Disciple-Making*. Grand Rapids: Zondervan Publishing House, 1978.

Eyres, Lawrence R. *The Elders of the Church*. Phillipsburg: P&R Publishing, 1975.

Finzel, Hans. *The Top Ten Mistakes Leaders Make*. Colorado Springs: Victon Books, 1994.

Henrichsen, Walter A. *Disciples are Made, Not Born*. Wheaton: Victor Books, 1988.

Hollingsworth, Mary. *Fireside Stories of Love, Life, and Laughter*. Nashville: Word Publishing, 2000.

Hull, Bill. *The Disciple-Making Pastor*. Old Tappan: Baker Publishing Group, 1988.

Hybels, Bill. *Courageous Leadership*. Grand Rapids: Zondervan Publishing House, 2002.

Bibliography

Jefferson, Charles. *The Minister as Shepherd*. Fincastle: Scripture Truth Books Co., 1991.

Kent, Homer A. *The Pastor and His Work*. Winnea Lake: BMH Books, 1963.

Laney, J. Carl. *A Guide to Church Discipline*. Minneapolis: Bethany House, 1985.

Lewis, C. S. *The Screwtape Letters*. Uhrichsville: Barbour & Company, Inc., 1990.

Lockyer, Herbert. *All the Apostles of the Bible*. Grand Rapids: Zondervan Publishing House, 1972.

MacArthur, John F. *Rediscovering Pastoral Ministry*. Dallas: West Publishing Group, 1995.

———. *Shepherdology*. Valencia: The Master's Fellowship, 1989.

———. *The Master's Plan for the Church*. Chicago: Moody Press, 1991.

Mack, Wayne A., and David Swavely. *Life in the Father's House*. Phillipsburg: P&R Publishing, 1996.

Maxwell, John C. *Developing the Leader Within You*. Nashville: Thomas Nelson Publishers, 1993.

———. *Irrefutable Laws of Leadership*. Nashville: Thomas Nelson Publishers, 1998.

Pentecost, J. Dwight. *Design for Discipleship*. Grand Rapids: Lamplighter Books, 1971.

———. *Designed to Be Like Him*. Chicago: Moody Press, 1976.

Robertson, Roy. *The Timothy Principle*. Colorado Springs: NavPress, 1986.

Russell, Bob. *When God Builds a Church*. West Monroe: Howard Publishing Company, Inc., 2000.

Sanders, J. Oswald. *Spiritual Leadership*. Chicago: The Moody Bible Institute of Chicago, 1994.

Scipione, George C. *Timothy, Titus, & You*. Phillipsburg: P&R Publishing, 1976.

Shelley, Marshall. *Well-Intentioned Dragons*. Minneapolis: Bethany Press International, 1984.

Stowell, Joseph M. *Shepherding the Church*. Chicago: Moody Press, 1997.

Strobel, Lee. *Inside the Mind of the Unchurched Harry and Mary*. Grand Rapids: Zondervan, 1993.

Sugden, Howard F., and Warren W. Wiersbe. *Confident Pastoral Leadership*. Chicago: Moody Press, 1973.

Taylor, Dr. and Mrs. Howard. *The Spiritual Secret of Hudson Taylor*. New Kensington: Whitaker House Publishers, 1996.

Thomas, Eugene. *The Hymnal for Worship & Celebration*. Waco: Word Music.

Unknown. *All About Following Jesus*. http://www.allaboutfollowingjesus.org/livingsacrifice.htm (accessed November 20, 2008).

———. *Leadership U*. http://www.leaderu.com/orgs/bpf/pathways/commit.html (accessed November 20, 2007).

Wallace, Daniel B. *Greek Grammar—Beyond the Basics*. Grand Rapids: Zondervan Publishing House, 1996.

Warren, Rick. *The Purpose-Driven Church*. Grand Rapids: Zondervan , 1995.

Watson, G. D. *awildernessvoice.com*. http://awildernessvoice.com/highcalling.html (accessed November 2007, 2008).

Bibliography

Wesley, John. *ThinkExist.com.* http://thinkexist.com/quotation/catch_on_fire_with _enthusiasm_and_people_will/212431.html (accessed November 20, 2007).

White, Kathleen. *Jim Elliott.* Minneapolis: Bethany House Publishers, 1990.

Men With a Mission

Training the Men God has Given You

DR. H. WALLACE WEBSTER

Training others is a serious call, and one we cannot ignore. Maybe you're not sure how to get started. Here's a proven method developed by the author of *Christ Will Build His Church*.

A three-year program has been built to produce qualified leaders in your church. Each year has a completed set of student material, teacher material, and PowerPoint slides. There's no need for you to reinvent the right material. Between the Word of God and *Men with a Mission*, you have just what you need.

Go to www.mabcmd.org and download the material today. It's ready for your immediate use. Why would you wait?

To order the *Men with a Mission*
student material, teacher material,
and PowerPoint slides, go to:
www.mabcmd.org
or contact

Mount Airy Bible Church
16700 Old Frederick Road
Mount Airy, MD 21771
E-mail: office@mabcmd.org
Toll-free: 1-877-489-4321